How to be a graphic designer, without losing your soul
Adrian Shaughnessy

Princeton Architectural Press, New York

Published in 2005 by
Princeton Architectural Press
37 East Seventh Street
New York, New York 10003

For a free catalog of books,
call 1.800.722.6657.
Visit our web site at www.papress.com.

Published simultaneously by
Laurence King Publishing Ltd, London

For Princeton Architectural Press:
Project editor: Nicola Bednarek

Special thanks to: Nettie Aljian, Dorothy Ball, Janet Behning, Megan Carey,
Penny (Yuen Pik) Chu, Russell Fernandez, Jan Haux, Clare Jacobson,
John King, Mark Lamster, Nancy Eklund Later, Linda Lee, Katharine Myers,
Lauren Nelson, Molly Rouzie, Jane Sheinman, Scott Tennent, Jennifer Thompson,
Joseph Weston, and Deb Wood of Princeton Architectural Press –
Kevin C. Lippert, publisher.

Library of Congress Cataloging-in-Publication Data

Shaughnessy, Adrian.
  How to be a graphic designer without losing your soul / Adrian Shaughnessy.
     p. cm.
  Includes bibliographical references.
  ISBN 1-56898-559-2 (alk. paper)
  1. Graphic arts–Vocational guidance. 2. Commercial art–Vocational guidance. I. Title.
  NC1001.S53 2005
  741.6'023–dc22

                                                      2005006488

Typeset in Berthold Akzidenz Grotesk

Printed in China

Seeing comes before words.

John Berger,
Ways of Seeing

How to be a graphic designer, without losing your soul

Contents

Foreword *Stefan Sagmeister*

I love being a designer. I love thinking about ideas freely and observing them taking shape; I love working concentratedly on a project all day, losing myself in the work, and, even after having been involved in this field for almost twenty years, I still love getting a piece back from the printer (if it turned out well).

There are so many fantastic designers working today: creators like Jonathan Barnbrook and Nicholas Blechman who emphasize the social role of design; designers who produce breathtaking forms, such as M/M in Paris, Nagi Noda in Tokyo and Mark Farrow in London; designers who blur the boundaries between design and technology like John Maeda, Joachim Sauter and their students; and a new generation who manage to work with one foot in the art world and the other in the design world, like the young Swiss group Benzin and the American designers involved in the 'Beautiful Losers' exhibition, including Ryan McGinness and Shepard Fairey.

I recently taught the spring/summer semester at the University of the Arts in Berlin, and was happy (and a bit astonished) to see how smart the students were. They are better educated, more widely travelled and more culturally astute than my generation was. On the same note, the range of students I currently teach in the graduate design program at New York's School of Visual Arts includes a biology major from Harvard and a senior designer from Comedy Central.

There is also a new emphasis on how design is reviewed and critiqued, driven by Steven Heller's *Looking Closer* series, *Emigre* magazine's reconfigured essay-heavy format, Rick Poynor's *No More Rules* and *Obey the Giant,* and maybe most significantly, by the emergence of design blogs like underconsideration.com and designobserver.com. i don't think there ever was a time when design was reviewed so critically and enthusiastically by so many people in so many cultures.

Of course, as it became a wider discipline, graphic design became more difficult. It now embraces what used to be a dozen different professions: my students compose music, shoot and edit film, animate and sculpt. They build hardware, write software, print silkscreen and offset, take photographs and illustrate. It's easy to forget that routine jobs like typesetting and color separation used to be separate careers. A number of schools have realized this and opened up the traditional boundaries between graphics, product design, new media, architecture and film/video departments, encouraging the education of a truly multi-faceted designer.

For me, it has become more difficult, too: as I get older I have to resist repeating what I've done before; resist resting on old laurels. Before the studio opened in 1993, I was working at M&Co., my then favorite design company in New York. When Tibor Kalman decided to close up shop in order to work on *Colors* magazine in Rome, it didn't feel right to go and work for my *second favorite* design company. So I opened my own studio and concentrated on my other great interest, music. I had experience working for both tiny and gigantic design companies and having enjoyed the former much more than the latter, I tried hard not to let the studio grow in size.

I feel a lot of designers starting out want to be concerned only with design and find questions about business and money bothersome. The proper set-up of a studio and the presentation of a project to a client – in short, the ability to make a project happen – is, of course, as much part of the design process (and much more critical to the quality of the process and the end product) as choosing ink colors or typefaces.

I learned a lot from my time at M&Co. They used time sheets, for example, and I thought, if it's not too square for them, it can't be wrong for me. I am glad I did too; it's the only way to find out if we made or lost money on a project. If I'm not on top of the financial details, they will soon be on top of me and I won't have a design studio any more. It is much cheaper to sit on the beach and read a book than it is to run a financially unsuccessful design studio.

Everything else about running a studio I learned from a book called *The Business of Graphic Design.* A pragmatic business book giving reasons why you should or shouldn't start your own company, it talked about how to design a business plan and estimate overheads. It described the advantages of both setting up alone and of partnerships.

I was also influenced by Quentin Crisp, now – sadly – remembered mainly as the subject of Sting's song *An Englishman in New York.* He talked to one of my classes, and he was such an inspiring character. Among the many smart things he said was: 'Everybody who tells the truth is interesting.' So I thought: this is easy, just try to be open and forthright, and it will be interesting.

I recently took a year off from clients. I used the time to make up my mind about all the fields I did not want to get into (but had previously imagined I would). I surprised myself by getting up every day at 6 am to conduct little type experiments (without a looming deadline). It made me think a lot about clients. I decided that I would rather have an educated client than one I have to educate. Tibor's line was that he would only take on clients smarter than him (but remember, a client does not have to be design literate to be smart). After reopening, I also decided to widen the scope of our studio to include four distinct areas: design for social causes, design for artists, corporate design and design for music.

So how does a graphic designer avoid losing his or her soul? Having misplaced little pieces of mine, I'm not sure if I am the right person to answer this question. What soul I have left I've managed to keep by pausing; by stopping and thinking. In my regular day-to-day mode, I get so caught up in the minutiae that I have little time or sense to think about the larger context. Because I used to work in different cities, a natural gap occurred between jobs, allowing for some reflection. When I got tired of moving and decided to stay put in New York, I created those gaps artificially by taking my year off or by teaching for a semester in Berlin. But even three days out of the office, alone, in a foreign city can do the trick.

I hope this book helps young designers find their way. I don't think that the 'designers don't read' bullshit is true. A good book will find good readers.

Poster
by Stefan Sagmeister

How to be a graphic designer, without losing your soul

This is Real Art
by Adrian Shaughnessy

To paraphrase Frank Zappa: here's just what the world needs – another graphic design book. Graphic design books are nearly as common as celebrity diet books or airport blockbusters. But for the committed designer there are few better ways to spend an hour than immersed in the pages of a luscious design book – we enjoy the bug-eyed envy that comes from looking at work we wish we'd done ourselves, and we are inspired by the dizzying range of graphic expression on view. And of course, as much as we enjoy the work, we also like to find fault with it. Moaning is important to designers; it's something we do well. But although design books can sometimes be accused of contributing to the widely held misconception that design is an effortless activity practised by star designers who never break sweat as they glide from triumph to triumph, they are, on the whole, *a good thing.*

And yet there's something missing in this encyclopedic coverage of design. When we gorge ourselves on the succulent work in the books, and when we slurp through the numerous magazines and websites that chronicle the design scene, we rarely get the back-story; we rarely get the grubby bits that go with almost every job touched by a graphic designer. Designers are quick to tell us about their sources of inspiration ('I'm really into Otl Aicher's pictograms and I like this beetroot-flavored chewing-gum wrapper I brought back from Osaka.'), but they are much less willing to reveal tiresome matters such as how they find clients, how much they charge and what they do when their client rejects three weeks of work and refuses to pay the bill. If you want to learn how to be a designer, you need to know about these and other messy matters. It's as much a part of being a designer as knowing how to kern type or design the perfect letterhead. In fact, how you deal with the grubby bits is how you learn to be a graphic designer.

Stefan Sagmeister's book *Made You Look* is one of the few design books that attempts to show a warts-and-all picture of the working life of a designer. He reproduces his failures ('the bad stuff') as well as his triumphs, he itemizes the fees he received, and in a pictorial cartoon reveals that even superstar designers have their work tampered with by meddlesome clients.

This is a book about the grubby bits. It is written by a designer *for* designers. It combines practical advice and philosophical guidance to help the independent-minded graphic designer deal with the less glamorous and knottier problems encountered by the working designer. I've added the phrase 'without losing your soul' to the book's title (I toyed with the idea of using 'shirt' instead of 'soul') because it seemed the best way to emphasize a key aspect of my intention: namely, to write a book designed to help those who believe that graphic design has a cultural and aesthetic value beyond the mere trumpeting of commercial messages; a book for those who believe that we become graphic designers because we are attracted to the act of personal creation; and a book for those who believe that design is at its best when the designer's voice is allowed to register, and is not suppressed in favor of blandness and sameness (although I should add that this is only relevant when the designer's voice is worth hearing).

This book is also a response to the fact that more people than ever are studying and practising graphic design. It is an increasingly attractive career. Where once it was seen as a purely artisanal occupation with not much status attached to it, it is now regarded as a meaningful, even mildly glamorous activity. Today, you can say that you are a graphic designer without people looking at you as if you've just announced that you do nude salsa dancing. Fashion designers, architects and product designers are already part of the new cultural elite: Tom Ford, Frank Gehry and Jonathan Ive are frequently interviewed with breathless reverence in newspapers, magazines and on television. And although graphic designers are not yet regarded with such slack-jawed wonder, David Carson, Peter Saville, Stefan Sagmeister, Neville Brody and a few others have a star rating that lifts them into the lower reaches of the celebrity designer cosmos. (At a guess graphic designers are seen as occupying a position in the media jungle somewhere between cable-TV game show hosts and tabloid journalists.)

2 This report, among others, can be found at www.bls.gov/oco/ocos090.stm

According to a recent US Department of Labor report,[2] there are 532,000 designers employed in the United States; 212,000 of these are graphic designers. In her book, *The Substance of Style,* Virginia Postrel points out that at least fifty graphic design magazines are regularly published around the world (there were three in 1970); and she quotes Pentagram partner and noted design commentator Michael Bierut: 'There's no such thing as an un-designed graphic object anymore, and there used to be.'

However, despite all this graphic abundance, most of the design that surrounds us lacks emotional character or aesthetic value. It's just there; clogging up the arteries of our visual lives. As the designer Paula Scher (also of Pentagram), noted in a 1994 essay published in the *AIGA Journal:* 'Everyday I find myself in supermarkets, discount drugstores, video shops, and other environments that are obviously untouched by our community … just plain old-fashioned non-controversial bad design, the kind of anonymous bad design that we've come to ignore because we're too busy fighting over the aesthetics of the latest AIGA poster.'[3] The prevalence of 'bad design' is a consequence of an increasingly competitive and globalized economy, where risk is anathema, where the herd instinct predominates and where sameness is the default position. It is unthinkable today that a powerful global brand would employ a contemporary designer in the way that IBM once employed Paul Rand, or that a commercial magazine sold on the newsstands would grant the freedom *The Face* gave Neville Brody in the 1980s. Focus groups and marketing imperatives would smother such initiatives at birth.

3 'The Devaluation of Design by the Design Community.' *AIGA Journal,* New York, 1994. Reprinted in Robyn Marsack, *Essays on Design 1: AGI's Designers of Influence* (London: Booth-Clibborn Editions), 1997.

Design itself is now intensely competitive; so much so, in fact, that many designers have become browbeaten into timidity and compliance. This is hardly surprising, since it's hard to take a stand on matters of principle when there are countless other firms and individuals willing to do the work if you don't. But, hang on, what's so bad about giving clients what they want? Isn't design a service industry?

This takes us to the heart of one of the most important debates in design over recent years. On the one hand, we have those who believe that graphic design is a problem-solving, business tool and that designers should suppress their desire for personal expression to ensure maximizing the effectiveness of the content. While on the other hand, we have those who believe that although design undoubtedly has a problem-solving function, it also has a cultural and aesthetic dimension, and its effectiveness is enhanced, and not diminished, by personal expression.

The former remains the dominant view amongst professional designers. But this traditionalist view of graphic design has always been subjected to critical attack and skepticism by radical voices in design, especially since the anti-globalization movement threw down a challenge to corporate behemoths in the late 1990s. And this pragmatic view of the designer's role doesn't hold true in other areas of design: we don't ask architects or fashion designers to suppress their personal voices – quite the opposite. In fact, we value most those who are capable of investing their work with personal statements. Nor, paradoxically, does the pragmatic view seem to have a basis in commercial reality. Increasingly, the messages that get noticed – the ones that cut through the drizzle of unremarkable one-size-fits-all communications – are the ones where the designer's thumbprint is clearly visible: the ones that contain a rebel-yell of defiance.

Nor is this schism as simple as a mere divergence between conservatives and radicals. If you read the design press you might think that the desire for creative freedom, or self-expression, was confined to superstar designers: it's not, it's actually universal. We become graphic designers because we want to say something. We want to make a visual statement for which we can stake a claim for authorship; in some cases it is a very modest claim, but it's a claim nonetheless. And even for those designers who fervently subscribe to the notion that the designer's contribution is always subservient to the client's needs and wishes, these individuals still want to perform this function their way. Let me put it another way: I don't think I've ever met a designer who didn't have the instinct for self-expression. You can see it in the universal reluctance to have ideas rejected, tampered with or watered down. There's a mule-like instinct in nearly every designer – even the most accommodating and service-minded – that bristles at the command 'Oh, can you change that' and the 'Just do it like this' attitude so frequently adopted by design's paymasters – the clients. It's an instinct, inherent in all designers, that says: a little bit of my soul has gone into this and it is not going to be removed without a fight.

The situation is further complicated by the fact that all graphic designers agree that there are, unquestionably, purely practical and utilitarian roles for graphic design. Applications such as road signs, medicine packaging, timetables and the presentation of financial, scientific or technical data, require design of the utmost clarity and precision. It is broadly agreed that there is no room in this sphere for notions such as personal expression or experimentation. A badly designed road sign might kill you: death by typography is a real possibility. And yet, show me a designer who doesn't want to execute even these tasks in the way he or she sees fit?

To arrive at a definition of what this book will tell you, it might be easier to say what this book will *not* tell you. This book will not tell you how to work the trapping functions in QuarkXpress. It will not tell you anything about hardware, software or the minutiae of Apple's latest operating system. There are countless books on these subjects, and in my experience designers learn these skills only when they need to, and they learn them from other designers or by working them out for themselves.

This book doesn't tell you what sort of designer you should be. In matters of styles, trends and schools of design, this book is agnostic. It will not tell you what typefaces are cool nor what the current trends in layout, photography and illustration are. It will not advocate the supremacy of formal design over vernacular design, or the desirability of Helvetica over Bodoni. You can get this information by looking at books and magazines, by reading about graphic design history, by talking to other designers and by experimentation within your own work. And although the great Josef-Müller Brockmann said 'All design work has a political character,' this book assumes that political questions are a matter for individual consciences. If, for instance, you are asked to design the packaging for a canned drink which contains dubious chemicals, you have a moral decision to make. Your conscience might tell you not to do this work, but if you are struggling to pay your bills, or have a family and financial commitments, you will find it hard to say no. This book doesn't tell you what to do in this situation: only you can make the decision.

Nor does this book tell you how to file your tax returns, prepare management accounts or deal with the complexities of employment law. There are much better equipped writers than me to tell you these things (a bibliography and appendix are provided at the back of this book), and in my experience, designers are, as a rule, not interested in this sort of information and also not very good at absorbing it until they have to. However, if you are going to survive – either as a freelance designer or by running a small studio – you are going to have to know about these things. So, rather than tell you how to do these things, I am going to tell you how to find accountants and other professional advisers to do them for you.

Interview in *Eye* 19, Winter 1995

In America, the aptly named *How* magazine covers practical issues relating to professional practice, with many useful articles on the less glamorous aspects of life as a designer, often written by practising designers. In the UK, *Design Week*, which claims to be the world's only weekly design magazine, regularly devotes space to practical matters.

I think the reader is now entitled to ask, well, what *does* this book tell me about? It gives the answers to some questions that designers ask themselves repeatedly. The urge to write this volume came from speaking to – and more importantly, listening to – students and young working designers. As a frequent visitor to design schools, I am asked questions such as: 'How do you respond to crap briefs?'; 'How do you stop clients demanding unreasonable changes to your work?'; 'How do you find interesting work?' I hear similar questions when I talk to designers who've been in practice for two or three years: 'How do you do good work and make money?'; 'How do you stop clients changing your work?'; 'How do you avoid spending your whole life doing unpaid pitches for low-budget work?'

It occurred to me that here was a stratum of questions – a mixture of the practical and the philosophical – that graphic designers found hard to get answers to. The art schools are preoccupied with producing 'broadly based' graduates and have insufficient time to prepare students for every aspect of working life. The glossy design press devotes its energies to chronicling the work of the latest hot designers, but avoids the practical issues facing working designers. Design writing and critical discourse rarely touch on the practicalities of life as a designer. And as more and more designers emerge from higher education only to be faced with the realization that there are not enough jobs to go round, designers are having to acquire levels of entrepreneurial determination that previous generations didn't need until much later in their careers. 'How to be a graphic designer …' sets out to fill some of these gaps and offers advice and guidance that suit the sensibilities of independent-minded designers.

The US writer and designer Kenneth Fitzgerald touched on this subject in an *Eye* magazine article titled 'Fanfare for the Common Hack' (*Eye* 27, Spring 1998), in which he urged theorists not to turn a deaf ear to 'down-in-the-trenches' designers.

So who is this book aimed at? You might say that this is a book for designers who accept design's conventional role, but who also see a parallel role for design as a culturally and socially beneficial force. If you want to narrow the book's focus still further, I'd say it is a practical and philosophical guide for students emerging, or about to emerge, from higher education and for working designers in the early stages of their careers. It is first and foremost a book for the free thinking designer.

But who am I to tell you about these matters? I am a self-taught graphic designer. I started out as a trainee in a big studio in the pre-digital era. I was informally apprenticed to a group of experienced designers who taught me the basics of typography, showed me how to prepare mechanical artwork, gave me a CMYK color percentages chart, and left me to get on with it. This was daunting, but it was also my lucky break. I'd been a bit of a slacker up until this point. But within a few weeks I was producing acceptable commercial design and artwork, and as a reward I was given a full-time job as a junior designer. You could say that graphic design saved my life.

Until recently I was creative director of a design company called Intro. I co-founded the company in 1988 with my then business partner Katy Richardson. We won awards and built up a small but steadily growing reputation in the UK and abroad, as a reliable, well-run and inventive design company. Our clients were an assortment of record labels, blue-chip corporations, arts organizations, educational bodies and media companies; we even had the British National Health Service as a client and managed to produce effective work for them, while also working for bands like Primal Scream and Stereolab. We were early proponents of the new cross-media approach to graphic design; we were among the first companies in the digital era to combine design and film-making (digital and traditional) under the same roof, something that has become more common since.

As the company grew (we were forty-strong at one giddy point) I did less and less design. As creative director, I was involved in finding and developing young designers, and acting as the bridge between our designers and our clients. I discovered a talent for advocacy, and I learned that communication skills are one of the most valuable skills a designer can have. In December 2003 I left Intro and set up as a freelance art director, writer and consultant. At Intro we came as close as is possible in a tough and unforgiving world to being a profitable (although not rich) design company that also did ground-breaking work. Our combination of creativity underpinned by business rigor worked well; but it was hard graft, and after fifteen years I began to feel the strain. Intro continues to prosper and do excellent work.

The book also contains contributions from leading designers. In a series of interviews they reveal their approaches to common problems faced by young designers making decisions early in their careers; you'll find elegant and insightful contributions from a cross-section of talented individuals including Neville Brody of Research Studios, Rudy VanderLans of Emigre, Natalie Hunter of Airside, John Warwicker of Tomato, Peter Stemmler of quickhoney and e-boy, Angela Lorenz, among others.

A final word before we start: you can ignore every piece of advice contained in these pages and still become a successful and fulfilled designer. All my advice comes with an override button: there is no such thing as a set of rules that will turn you into the complete graphic designer. In my vision of how to be a graphic designer there is always room for the maverick, the difficult and the downright contrary. I'm not trying to create homogenized designers. Far from it: what I want to do is provide the reader with a series of clues, hints and prompts to help make working life more enjoyable and rewarding. I want to talk about subjects that are not often discussed, and matters that are 'assumed' to be understood, but which rarely are. I want to help you avoid making the mistakes that I made. I want to help you become an effective and self-reliant graphic designer – without losing your soul along the way.

Chapter 1 / p.17–27
Attributes needed by the modern designer *'Graphic design is for self-centered obsessives'* A discussion of the main creative, philosophical and practical attributes required by the contemporary graphic designer.

Among the myriad definitions of graphic design, one of the most illuminating is by the American designer and writer Jessica Helfand. According to Helfand, graphic design is a 'visual language uniting harmony and balance, color and light, scale and tension, form and content. But it is also an idiomatic language, a language of cues and puns and symbols and allusions, of cultural references and perceptual inferences that challenge both the intellect and the eye.'[1]

I like Helfand's definition. Her first sentence is a conventional summary of graphic design; few would argue with it. But her second sentence throws a punch: it alludes to design's expressive power and higher intent. Even as a recalcitrant teenager I sensed graphic design's emotive potency. I didn't even know there was such a thing as graphic design, but I lovingly copied lettering from album covers, magazines, cereal boxes and comic books. I didn't copy other elements; only the lettering. I liked the way that particular letterforms gave words added meaning. I noticed that the same words in a different typeface were not necessarily as beguiling. Copying letterforms is a common enough occupation among bored teenagers – it seems to have a calming effect on turbulent hormones: it was used memorably as a trope for disaffected youth by Geoff McFetridge in his title sequence for Sofia Coppola's film The Virgin Suicides.

As with many designers, album covers provided me with a link between an embryonic visual awareness and the discovery of graphic design.[2] I was mesmerized by the imagery I found on record sleeves, and before long I started noticing the design credits on album covers. This led to the realization that there was something called graphic design (I'm not sure I'd have got it from any other source) – and it seemed like a pretty cool occupation. Today, graphic design is far less mysterious. You can study it at school, and any kid with a computer discovers fonts, layout and image manipulation at about the same time as they learn to stop using a diaper.

[1] Quoted by Virginia Postrel in The Substance of Style (New York: Harper Collins), 2003.

[2] The number of contemporary graphic designers who cite album covers as providing the impetus to take up graphic design is legion: the California-based designer and musician Tom Recchion is typical. In a recent article he wrote: 'King Crimson's first cover astonished me and forced me to buy it as an expensive import without hearing a note.' ('The Inner Sleeve,' The Wire 248, October 2004). It confirms album cover design as an enduring and substantial factor in design, and yet music graphics have not been treated by educators and the design establishment, with the same respect or degree of seriousness normally reserved for other forms of design.

Cultural Awareness

The second part of Helfand's definition provides the key to producing meaningful and expressive graphic design: 'cues and puns and symbols and allusions, of cultural references and perceptual inferences' are the elements that give work authority and resonance. And if you want to introduce these elements into your work, it means taking an interest in everything that goes on around you, and having curiosity about areas other than graphic design: politics, entertainment, business, technology, art, ten-pin bowling and mud wrestling.

This cultural awareness (you can call it research, if you like, but it's really something larger) ranks higher than technical ability and academic qualifications in the designer's portfolio of attributes. When the British writer Iain Sinclair was asked if he did research for his books, he replied that his whole life was research. I can't think of a better adage for the modern graphic designer. Without constantly scanning, scrutinizing and absorbing what goes on around you, you cannot become a successful designer. This was brought home to me a few years ago at a design seminar in Hong Kong that I took part in. After presentations by a number of British designers, there was a lively Q&A session. Someone in the audience asked me if I'd like to work for clients in Hong Kong. I said yes – mainly out of politeness, but also because I thought it was the answer the audience expected to hear. Then I thought about it: I was kidding myself. I've only been in Hong Kong for twenty-four hours, I don't speak the language, my knowledge of the place's history and customs is slight, to say the least, and yet here I am presuming to think that I can create meaningful design. But, most chastening of all was the realization that I'd spent the previous hour demonstrating to the audience how my company's design work was stuffed with subtle cultural allusions – things that you had to be culturally savvy to spot. How could I achieve the same in Hong Kong without study, research and knowledge of the culture?

Frames from the title
sequence of *The Virgin Suicides*
by Geoff McFetridge

Cultural awareness is vital for the modern designer, and most designers are culturally aware people. It's why designers are often witty with a sophisticated sense of humor (we shouldn't be surprised at this: designers are observers, and the best humor comes from microscopic observation). Take Peter Saville's CD cover design for the band Gay Dad. Saville is not generally thought of as a graphic humorist, but his clever appropriation of the silhouette of the 'little green man' from the walk sign, for the cover of a CD by a rock band, is unexpected and amusing. Everyone knows this symbol. In fact, it's so familiar we barely notice it. Yet it takes a graphic designer's sly wit to extract it from the mundane environment and place it in this unlikely setting. Witty, you might say.

3   The designer Lorraine Wild describes the benefits of understanding the 'larger context' in which her work is situated: 'I used to do more research and now I'm more intuitive. I've gotten better at understanding the materials that I'm given to work with by writers, editors, curators, artists and architects, etc. I have always been conscientious about knowing the material, but now I've accumulated a library in my head which helps me read the larger context that surrounds the subject I'm about to work with …' Lorraine Wild, 'Reputations,' Eye 36, Summer 2000.

I once read that safe-crackers rub the tips of their fingers with sandpaper to increase tactile sensitivity. It makes their fingertips ultra-sensitive and enables them to feel the nuances of the lock's gear mechanism, as they rotate the dial in search of the magic combination that will open the safe. It's the same with graphic design: the more sensitive you become to the world around you the better you will function. This means studying design in all its contemporary manifestations, as well as design history and the visual arts in general. But it also means studying the world beyond graphic design. Designers sometimes imagine that the world revolves around graphic design, and when you are working fourteen-hour days it's hard to remember that it doesn't. But the best designers have a healthy interest in life beyond their subject; design may be their main concern, and it may provide them with a consuming and stimulating career, but it doesn't eclipse other interests. [3]

I know what you're thinking: you're thinking, Okay, but how does this help me become a better designer and get my work accepted? Here's how: the single most important thing you can do when discussing a job with a new or potential client is to demonstrate understanding, openness and receptivity. The designer who shows only signs of self-absorption and narrowness of focus isn't going to inspire his or her client. It might seem obvious, but it's surprising how many designers use meetings with clients to talk about themselves and their work. These are often the same designers who complain that their work is frequently rejected or that they are never allowed to 'do what they want to do.' Hardly surprising. They are guilty of the worst crime a graphic designer can commit: they are revealing themselves to be self-centered and to have a narrow outlook. For the ambitious designer, this is fatal.

If you can demonstrate some knowledge about the client's field of activity, if you can talk about the project at hand and if you can listen instead of prattling on about yourself, you will be astonished at how receptive your new client will be to you and your ideas. It's a rich paradox, but the less you make a client/designer relationship about yourself, the more it will tip in your favor. Try it, it works.

Of course, it isn't always enough to rely on knowledge. You need to back it up with specific research. I once turned up at a meeting with the managers of an art gallery who were looking for a new design company. Arrogantly, I didn't do any research. I relied on a shaky notion of who I thought my potential client was. In fact, I'd got them mixed up with another gallery. When my mistake was exposed I got a frosty response and, needless to say, I didn't get the gig.

Communication

As well as possessing cultural awareness and being aware of the world beyond graphic design, the modern designer needs to be a skilled communicator. This is not the same as being able to make eloquent speeches at design conferences. Rather, it is about possessing the ability to talk about your work, especially with clients and non-designers, in a coherent, convincing and objective way, without resorting to the language and idioms that you'd use with other designers. And since communication is a two-way street, it is also about listening.

Graphic design is a non-verbal medium. Graphic design is expected to communicate without the benefit of written or spoken commentaries describing the designer's intentions: you can't stand beside your poster in the street drawing attention to your subtle use of Akzidenz and pointing out its mute evocation of Modernist rationality and truthfulness, can you? Yet designers need words: and they rarely need them as much as when they are presenting new work. As Norman Potter notes in his seminal text *What is a Designer:* 'This aspect of design work is frequently underestimated: an ability to use words clearly, pointedly, and persuasively is at all times relevant to design work.'[4]

Norman Potter, *What is a Designer* (London: Hyphen Press), 2002.

4

Persuading clients that your ideas are right and that their money is being spent wisely, requires huge amounts of carefully formulated argument. Presenting work to new clients, and to those clients who are not design literate, is among the most difficult tasks facing the designer. And surprisingly, considering its importance, designers are often not very good at talking about their own work. In a later chapter I'll discuss the finer points of making a good presentation (there's an art to it: think of it as the graphic designer's equivalent of the Japanese tea ceremony), but for now, I'll confine myself to making the point that knowing how to talk about your work is fundamental to becoming a successful designer.

To help designers develop verbal skills, I sometimes ask them to describe what they've done *before* they show me what they've done. I ask them to describe their work to such a degree of accuracy that it isn't necessary to actually see the work to know what they've done. It's a good exercise and worth trying out with your own work. At Intro, this ability to 'tell but not show' came in useful when I was told that an important new client had arrived in the building unexpectedly. 'I was just passing …' he said, 'thought I'd drop in to see how you were getting on.' My diary said that he wasn't due to visit us for another three days. And besides, our presentation wasn't ready – it wasn't even started. But he was one of these impatient clients who imagine that once they've briefed a designer, the designer does nothing else other than work on their project. I had a dilemma: should I tell him to go away, or talk to him about our ideas without showing him anything?

What is a Designer, Norman Potter, cover design by Françoise Berserik

Courtesy of Hyphen Press

Courtesy of Intro

Malcolm McLaren,
The Largest Movie House in Paris,
by Mat Cook at Intro

5   I have a long-standing
     music industry client
     (Daniel Miller of
     Mute Records), who
     invariably prefers
     'roughs' to the finished
     jobs. It's the same
     with music: he usually
     prefers the demo to
     the finished track.

I spoke to Mat Cook, the Intro designer working on the project. Mat looked at me calmly and said he could deal with it. We sat down with our client, and I watched, dry-mouthed, as Mat (an inspirational art director) described his intentions. He had an elaborate and ambitious plan to photograph an old-fashioned radiator in the middle of a block of ice; the heater was to be switched on and glowing at the heart of the frozen block. Mat described the image, slowly and methodically conjuring up a mental picture of the finished image, its setting and its likely effect on its intended audience. He did this with such vividness and confidence that our client approved the idea on the spot – without seeing anything. I don't recommend this as a universal strategy; it is usually better to have smart visual representations of your ideas, but it's a good demonstration of the merits of being able to talk effectively about your work.

The way designers present ideas is as important as the ideas themselves. When a good idea is rejected, it is often the presentation of that idea that is being rejected, not the idea itself. The dominance of the computer has meant that handmade layouts, and what were once called 'roughs' or 'visuals', are now largely redundant. We have lost the opportunity to 'sketch' ideas roughly;[5] where once clients would have been content with mocked-up approximations of the finished design, they now expect and demand to see the finished thing. Digital technology makes this possible, and life is made easier for the graphic designer. But not every idea can be executed in this way, and one of the consequences of this is that we find ourselves presenting only those ideas that we can comfortably mock up using our scanner and Photoshop. In other words, we avoid ideas that can't be easily executed by digital means: designers must not let technological capabilities define their thinking.

Yet if we want to present complex ideas like radiators in blocks of ice, it is often not sufficiently convincing to attempt to replicate the idea using sub-standard images cobbled together in Photoshop. Our attempts will not convince. If we can do away with the need to do inaccurate visuals by using language to describe our ideas, we can often save ourselves a great deal of heartbreak. Of course there is a danger that our client will get the wrong idea, so our language must be precise.

Spoken communication therefore is a vital component of the modern designer's kitbag. But there is a communication skill even more important than being able to talk convincingly about your work: listening. I'm talking about the acknowledgment that communication is a two-way street, and that your client has a point of view that you need to listen to carefully for clues and unspoken messages. If you could climb inside your client's head, you'd be astonished by what you'd find. You'd find someone fretting about spending money on something that he or she can't see or touch. Imagine going into a chic store and agreeing to buy a sofa that you aren't allowed to look at. You wouldn't do it. But that, roughly speaking, is what clients are asked to do when they buy design – especially from a new and untried graphic designer. They don't really know what they are buying until it is delivered. It makes hiring a designer difficult and leads to more unhappiness and failed jobs than any other factor. But by listening intently, you can often identify the factors that concern clients the most.

What we are really talking about is listening to the client's point of view. This is the first rule of communication for the graphic designer. Now, I know what you're thinking. Earlier I argued in favor of the designer developing and maintaining a personal voice. Well, I'm certainly not abandoning that view. But, if you want your opinions as a designer to be taken seriously, you have to allow your client to have an opinion too. In other words, there has to be a balance of interests. And that balance of interests usually has to be achieved through negotiation. It won't happen naturally. I recently saw an example of this inability to negotiate a balance between client and designer on a television program that followed an interior designer as she tried to design an apartment for a client. The client was arrogant and indecisive, the interior designer hesitant and easily bullied. Their professional relationship jumped the rails almost immediately. The interior designer's response to her client's unreasonable and fluctuating demands was to offer to 'keep showing you stuff until you are happy.' Big mistake.

So what should she have done? She should have listened to the brief and then responded with her ideas. If, at this stage, her client had remained indecisive and interfering, she had a choice – dump the client or insist on drawing up a new brief. She did neither, instead she offered to do 'whatever' her client wanted, and as a result an ugly and protracted meltdown ensued. The client ended up driving the project despite saying repeatedly that he didn't know anything about design, and the designer became angry and defeatist. Yet I blame the designer: she began correctly by allowing her client to have a point of view, but she forgot to have one herself – perhaps she never had one in the first place? All great work comes about when viewpoints are balanced: in other words, when both client and designer feel that they are being listened to. Achieve this – find the point of balance in a relationship – and you'll get results.

The designer Rudy VanderLans identifies another frequent problem in designer/client relationships. 'You have to listen very carefully to what the client wants,' notes VanderLans, 'and be careful not to approach the project with a preconceived idea of what it should look like. In my own experience, too often I approached a design job wanting to use a certain font or a particular typographic mannerism, simply because it's what I felt comfortable with at the time. But that wasn't always what the client wanted.'

This is a hot potato for the ambitious, independent-minded designer. Good designers have plenty of ideas and they're itching to use them. But it's a mistake, as VanderLans points out, to foist them on clients. It usually ends in tears – an unhappy client and a dissatisfied designer. Another frequent cause of breakdowns between client and designer is closely related to this problem: designers often make the mistake of saying to their clients: 'I've done it like this *because I like it.'* It is an understandable viewpoint; designers can't help putting their personal tastes and sensibilities into their work.

There's a great piece of archive film from the 1960s, in which a fierce-looking professor of music commands his viewers – in heavily European-accented English – to listen to the music of Pink Floyd. The band plays one of their meandering psychedelic album tracks and then joins the professor for an uncomfortable discussion. The professor, barely able to contain his epicurean disgust, asks them why their music has to be so loud. Bass-player Roger Waters good-naturedly replies: 'Because we like it' – and promptly loses the argument.

Designers use fonts, colors, layouts and imagery because they like them: it would be an odd designer who used design elements that he or she *didn't* like. Even when designers are being totally subservient to the brief, they still use styles and modes of expression that they personally like. It follows, therefore, that there is nothing wrong with doing things because you 'like' them. But there is something wrong with telling clients that this is what you've done; in fact, it's the worst thing you can say to a client. You might get away with it if you are a star designer, or if you have a cheerful trusting rapport with your client. But if you are establishing a new working relationship you have to be able to articulate a genuine rationale for your work.

I say genuine, because we're not talking about perfecting some sleazy 'customer relations' technique here. We are actually talking about confronting a familiar problem in design: we are talking about the frequent occurrence of designers making clients feel (rightly or wrongly) that designers are pleasing themselves at their client's expense. It's well known in advertising, for example, that winning industry awards is sometimes the primary concern of an agency's creative staff, and because of this, clients often accuse agencies of ignoring their needs in favor of creating work that appeals to the judges who sit on awards panels, usually fellow practitioners. The new managing director of a giant global brand recently caused a furor amongst UK advertising agencies when his comments about his company's advertising were reported in the British advertising journal *Campaign*: 'I don't like any of the ads …' he said, 'they are focused on awards, not on selling more product to more people at higher prices.'

I'm aware that it is hard for designers to be detached and objective when talking about their work. Designers often 'feel things' at a sub-verbal level, and are loath, or unable, to provide explanations for creative actions. Some well-known designers, capable of the most elegant and articulate work, are not much good at talking about what they do or explaining why they do it. But if you can learn to talk about your work – especially if you are not a paradigm-shifting design genius – and if you can find patterns of words that communicate meaning and value to clients, you will reap the benefits. And the easiest way to do this is to remove the personal from the equation. Do this and you'll find clients keener to accept your ideas and take your guidance: in other words, less you means more you.

I've talked a great deal about clients in this chapter: it's hard to avoid them. They share the terrain with us, so it's hardly surprising that they turn up everywhere. Self-initiated projects aside, no matter where you are in the graphic design landscape, you always have clients. If you work in a corporation you might report to a non-designer; if you work in a design studio you may report to a creative director or a senior designer, but they are all *clients* and how you treat them determines how they treat your work. For the ambitious designer, how to communicate with clients is the passport to good work, and it's worth becoming good at it.

Nor are clients the only people you have to communicate effectively with. You need to know how to talk to other designers. If you have designers as partners in a small business, or if you employ designers, then you have to be able to communicate with them in such a way that they don't feel cowed, threatened or discouraged by your views. You have to be able to talk to suppliers and collaborators. You will have to talk to IT people, bank mangers, tax officials and window cleaners.

How we do this depends on our personalities and our circumstances. In a profile of Canadian designer Bruce Mau and his studio, his communication skills were praised by Cathy Jonasson, Bruce Mau Design's vice-president and managing director. 'Bruce is demanding, but he's not prescriptive,' she says. Jonasson left a prestigious curatorial position at the Art Gallery of Ontario – and took a twenty per cent pay cut – to work for Mau's office. 'Mau is very good at looking at someone's work and finding the best in it. People leave him feeling good about their work and knowing what they have to do to make their work even better. He constantly emphasizes what you might call the "Mau method": Ask the right questions, understand the problem, and explore lots of possible solutions.'[7]

Scott Kirsner.
'Bruce Mau,'
Fast Company 39
[7] (October 2000).

Integrity

Integrity in design is a bit like obesity in ballet dancers – you don't often see it. This is not because designers lack honesty and decency; quite the opposite. Rather it is because preserving integrity in the remorseless climate of modern business is difficult. For designers, integrity often becomes a bargaining chip. We give it away in return for a job that comes with a lot of cash, or we hang onto it and do the work we want to do for little or no money. It is tough to retain integrity and make a living. But it's not impossible.

There are laws to prevent fraudulent practices. Specific offences such as copyright theft and malpractice in the workplace are punishable. Yet in the way that we conduct ourselves as designers, we are as free as the marketplace allows us to be. However, as a general rule, the designer who behaves morally will do better than the one who doesn't – if only because design is a social activity, with social consequences. Over the years, many professional design associations have attempted to draw up ethical codes. There is much to be said for these attempts to establish rules and guidelines for the proper conduct of designers. Unfortunately they tend to be undermined by shifts in public and business morality, or overtaken by rapid technological change.

In the 1971 edition of her book, *The Professional Practice of Design,* the British writer Dorothy Goslett wrote about the professional codes of conduct advocated by SIAD (the Society of Industrial Artists and Designers, now called the Chartered Society of Designers). She noted the following instruction: 'Now there is another Clause, Number 8, in the Code of Professional Conduct of the SIAD which may also have to be invoked during your first meeting with a possible client. This Clause reads: "A member (of the SIAD) shall not knowingly accept any professional assignment on which another designer has been or is working except with the agreement of the other designer or until he is satisfied that the former appointment has been properly terminated."'

This prohibition is charming and old-fashioned, and it is clearly untenable in the modern marketplace, where competition is valued above everything else. But is it so outmoded? I was talking to a designer friend recently and I mentioned that I'd heard that a large upmarket retailer in central London – a world-famous name – was looking for new designers to work on various projects. My friend said that he couldn't approach this client, because a designer friend of his already worked regularly for this retailer. I was struck by my friend's old-fashioned loyalty. This is what I mean when I talk about integrity: a personal philosophy which is not abandoned at the first sign of trouble.

Integrity, at its most earthbound, might be as simple as a love of design expressed in such a way that clients can see that, for you, design is something more than professional expediency. Alternatively, it might take a more practical form; it might be a refusal to take part in 'pitches.' Pitching is a hotly debated issue in contemporary design. Very few jobs of any size are assigned without a competitive pitch, and frequently these pitches are unpaid. As we've already noted, you are free to say no to these; many designers do. But in the post-Enron era of transparency in financial reporting, and new tendering rules in Europe, nearly all public bodies (and many firms) are obliged to offer contracts up to open tender to avoid accusations of corruption and mismanagement.

Whenever designers gather to discuss their profession, the subject of pitching arises; various professional bodies around the world have tried to formulate a correct response to the invitation by clients to pitch, but without much success. It is now so prevalent, that it is almost impossible to avoid taking part in it if you want to win bigger and more remunerative work. Yet the only way to do genuinely good work is for designer and client to form a partnership and explore all angles together in a mutually trusting and open way. This is not possible in a competitive pitch. No matter how good the brief, the designer is not addressing the client's requirements: he or she is merely taking part in a beauty parade. Regardless, clients derive a substantial benefit from being given – at no cost – a range of responses to their brief. This helps them to make and justify their final choice (they have something to evaluate it against), and in the case of unscrupulous clients (of which there are fewer than designers imagine) it affords them an opportunity to steal ideas. In other words, clients are receiving a quantifiable benefit that they do not pay for. Nor is it made any more excusable by designers' willingness to take part in pitches.

There is not much chance of pitching becoming any less common; in fact the opposite is happening, with even small projects being offered up for pitch. And laudable as it is to avoid corruption, designers who are expected to produce creative work without payment seem unduly penalized by this new drive for fiscal transparency. But by saying no to pitching, [8] studios and individuals are taking a principled stance – they might also be missing out on opportunities, but the respect they get from taking such a stance outweighs the occasional loss of business.

[8] Our policy at Intro was to participate in unpaid pitches if they opened doors that would otherwise remain closed to us. Because we weren't a conventional design group, we were often added to a pitch list as a wild card entry, so that the client could demonstrate that they had asked a variety of studios to compete. We used these opportunities to good advantage, often winning jobs by doing our homework as thoroughly as the others but also by bringing a freshness to what was new territory for us, and thereby exposing the formulaic nature of our more sector-experienced competitors. But, before agreeing to pitch, we always asked for a pitch fee (sometimes, to our surprise, we got one; sometimes we didn't). We insisted on knowing who we were pitching against and we made a friendly protest (through gritted teeth) about the inadvisability of pitches being the best way to commission design.

If we believe in nothing, then our clients will have no reason to believe in us. If we demonstrate the morals of the marketplace, then we will be treated like a commodity – and our services bought off at bargain basement prices. And here's an odd thing: in a world with no principles, people often respect those who have some.

Nor is it just in our work that we need to display integrity. We must have integrity in the way we deal with other designers, with suppliers (printers, programmers, technicians), and with people we meet in professional life. We must have integrity in the way we handle the creative work of other designers and creative people such as photographers and illustrators. Many of us will have been cavalier at some point in our working lives with typefaces, photographs or graphics software – but this is theft as surely as if we'd gone into someone's house and taken their possessions. We have to show integrity to the three 'audiences' for which design is most usually done: our clients, our intended audience and ourselves. Designers will differ on the order of importance in which they place this trinity: in my view, the demands and responsibilities of all three have to be equally balanced.

For Neville Brody, personal integrity in design is what differentiates the 'good from the bad'. And he's right. By standing up for yourself, by having beliefs (creative and ethical beliefs), and perhaps most importantly of all, by questioning what you are asked to do as a designer, you can acquire self-respect, which is the first step on the path to earning the respect of clients and other designers. You might also get the sack, but that's integrity for you – there's a price to be paid for it.[9] Just remember, it's always less than the price of your self-respect. I might even say, the price of your soul.

I promised you practical advice and up until now we've dealt only with rather lofty, abstract notions. In subsequent chapters we'll tackle more mundane matters. Yet without the attributes of cultural awareness, communication skills and professional and personal integrity, you are not going to grow as a designer. You will notice, thus far, I haven't mentioned the word 'talent'. You need talent to be a graphic designer, but talent in graphic design comes in myriad forms. There is no yardstick: no foolproof way of measuring it and it's one of the great joys of the craft of graphic design that it accommodates so many sorts of 'talent'. You don't have to be able to draw to be a great typographer, for example. Design is a very generous and accommodating matrix of opportunities, and yes, you will need talent to be a successful graphic designer, but a little talent can be made to go a long way if it is supported by the attributes listed above. Some designers are born with cultural awareness, communication skills and personal integrity, while others have to work to acquire them: this takes time and there are disappointments and setbacks along the way.

9 Peter Saville told the *Times* of London (15 September, 2004): 'The trouble with graphic design today is: when can you believe it? It's not the message of the designer anymore. Every applied artist ends up selling his or her soul at some point. I haven't done it and look at me. People call me one of the most famous designers in the world and I haven't got any money'.

Neville Brody

Neville Brody was born in London in 1957. He has been a key figure in graphic design for over two decades. Brody forged his reputation through his revolutionary work as art director for *The Face* magazine. In 1988 he published the first of two monographs. In 1994, Brody launched Research Studios, London, followed by studios in Paris and Berlin. Clients range across all media, from web to print, and from environmental and retail design to moving graphics and film titles. A sister company, Research Publishing, produces and publishes experimental multimedia works by young artists. He also organizes the FUSE Project, a renowned conference and quarterly publication centering on innovations in digital language.

www.researchstudios.com

Design
by Neville Brody

AS Tell me about your design education. NB I did a foundation course at Hornsey Art School which had been a militant hotbed of rebellion in the 1960s, but Margaret Thatcher closed it down when she became prime minister. She demolished mass social action and sold everything off to the highest bidder. After this, I went to the London College of Printing because it had a reputation for being strict and traditional. I wanted to learn my trade. I really believe in the apprenticeship idea.

In interviews you have said that you were accused of 'not being commercial'. How did the LCP equip you for working life? The only advice they gave me was to wear a tie to interviews. I left and went into four years of real poverty. People urged me to get a job in advertising – but I stuck to what I believed in. And if you believe in something you must do the same. Not getting a job doesn't mean that you are no good. Things will come round.

What inspired you to set up on your own and pursue your own ideas? When I started out I had a feeling that I could change things. There was a sense of revolution. People like Nick Logan (founder of *The Face*), and even people like Richard Branson, had this feeling that change was possible. Punk was a big liberator. Then along came Thatcher and Reagan and they said risk is dangerous. They sanitized society. They introduced genericism – standardized lifestyles. Their answer to anyone was if you feel depressed – go buy something. Today there is no equivalence to punk. It felt like anything was possible.

What's the difference between today's designers and your generation – the designers who came out of punk and post-punk? Young designers say they want their work to be seen. That's their message, that's their reason for doing something – to gain recognition. It wasn't mine, I had ideas that got picked up. I didn't start out to be famous, I started out with some ideas and a philosophy. Today, design has become about celebrity for celebrity's sake. But being a famous designer doesn't make you rich. You get fired by clients. And you sometimes have to fire clients.

What is your advice to a designer setting out in business today? If you have integrity, you say no to things. You must say no to things that are morally wrong. I wouldn't work for a tobacco company, for example. But I also believe in trying to work closely with clients. Microsoft dominates ninety per cent of the computer market – but by working for them, I'm saying the war is over. I want to try and get them to humanize their process. I've told them that they have to be a bottom-up – not a top-down company. So many big brands are now outdated. Digital distribution is changing everything; there is a new hunger – a post-branding generation that I have a great optimism about.

A final word? The main thing is to have personal integrity. It's what differentiates the good from the bad. Oh, and traditional graphic design ruined my eyesight.

They don't tell you this in design school, but the reason you go to school is to learn how to learn. No design school can do much more than this. But to be taught how to learn is pretty useful, because when you emerge after three, perhaps five years of hard study, [1] you go back to the beginning and start all over again. In my experience, a graduate fresh from school takes between six and eighteen months to become a contributing member of a studio – and that is with careful shepherding and plenty of attention. There are, occasionally, design graduates who emerge from full-time education as thoroughly grounded individuals ready to deal with professional life. But they are rare: it's safer to assume that you need to go back to the starting line and start all over again.

Everyone needs a job. We need a job to earn money to pay for shelter, food, books, music and other life-sustaining essentials. But for designers there is a far more important consideration: we need to start learning on the job; we need to gain experience. We need to start learning how to be a graphic designer.

How do you find that first job, and how do you know which one is right for you? The first thing to remember is that for a first job there are no wrong jobs. Even in the scummy places where you are treated like a schmuck, there are lessons to be learned and career firsts to be notched up. This is not the same as saying: I will accept the first job that comes along. Rather, it is saying: I need to build a robust personal philosophy of professional life, I need experience and I need to be working; and everything I see and touch makes me a better designer. If you already think like this, you can stop reading this chapter and skip ahead.

Few tasks will tax the fledgling designer more than finding a first job. It is an unfairly severe task to have to face at the outset of your career, when you are least equipped to deal with it. [2] Some people do it effortlessly; others take years to find their niche; a few never find theirs. But over the next few pages, I will provide pointers to help make the process of job hunting less difficult. It is worth mentioning that the two best designers I ever employed broke every rule I am about to give you: neither conducted themselves in their job interviews in a way I would recommend, yet both had qualities that shone through their lack of interview savvy; both exhibited a diamond-hard conviction that disarmed me, and against my rational judgment, convinced me to employ them. To make matters worse, both took an age to become effective, although ultimately they each turned out to be bona fide stars. My point here is that I believe there is nearly always a valid alternative way of doing everything, and if by doing things your own way and following your

[1] As the design writer Steven Heller noted in an article on the AIGA website (www.journal.aiga. org): 'Proficiency in requisite technologies, not to mention a slew of optional techniques, easily takes a year or more to master in a rudimentary way. Acquiring fluency in the design language(s), most notably type, is an ongoing process. Then there is instruction and practice in a variety of old and new media – print and web, editorial and advertising, static and motion, not to mention drawing and photography – these take time to learn, no less to hone. And what about the liberal arts: writing, history and criticism?

Theory is also a useful foundation if taught correctly, but it is often perfunctorily shoehorned into studio classes. How can a design student function without verbal expertise, let alone the ability to read and research? This must also be taught in an efficient manner that takes time. And then there is basic business acumen; every designer must understand fundamental business procedures, which are virtually ignored in the ultimate pursuit of the marketable portfolio.'

[2] The designer and blogger Armin Vit writes: 'Being a young graphic designer is not easy, physically or emotionally. We enter the field with talent, potential and personality as our primary assets at an age (average of 23) where we are not exactly kids anymore but surely not responsible adults yet.' 'The Young and Not So Restless' *Voice: AIGA Journal of Design* (4 June, 2004).

own instincts, you choose to travel down a different path, then go ahead. In a world of conformity, 'different' can be invigorating and as welcome as a drink of water to a traveller lost in the desert.

In this chapter we'll look at finding a job in an in-house studio within a corporation or institution, and we'll look at ways of landing a job in an independent design studio. We'll weigh up the pros and cons of each, and we'll discuss ways to approach both options.

Sometimes, when it comes to finding a job, the correct path is already chosen for you. If you want to be a magazine designer, for example, you will almost certainly have to take a job in a publishing house since most magazines are designed in-house, although there are some independent design studios that produce magazines for publishing-sector clients. The same might apply if you are interested in packaging; many retailers and manufacturers run in-house studios to produce their own packaging. Similarly, many businesses employ web designers in-house; broadcasters and television stations often have teams of moving-image designers; museums, galleries and cultural organizations typically employ large in-house teams.

'Working in-house' is often dismissed as an inferior option to working in an independent studio, but it can be equally rewarding. You learn about the world of business, you familiarize yourself with the conventions of the workplace and you gain an education that will stand you in good stead in later life if you set up on your own. You might also earn more money than if you work in an independent design studio, and you will enjoy a period of financial security at a time when you should be devoting all your energies to learning your craft and not being distracted by the problems that can afflict small design studios (bad debts, the grind of finding new work, punishing deadlines, etc.).

Design Week recently ran an article investigating the pros and cons of working in-house in the UK. It listed the benefits as: 'More civilised working hours … better work/life balance' and it listed the disadvantages as: 'Often located away from the urban design hubs … can have stigma attached.' [3] The English designer Chris Ashworth has worked on both sides of the fence. After graduating from design school, he set up his own studio. Subsequently, he worked for an independent design studio and MTV, before succeeding David Carson as art director of Raygun magazine. He is now creative director of Getty Images, the giant image library. Ashworth views both experiences as sharply contrasting. He compares independent studio life with working in-house by way of a series of contrasting adjectives: 'Instability, stability; isolation, interaction; freedom, collaboration; local, global; notes, briefs.'

When pressed to say if he had more freedom on his own, he replies enigmatically: 'Yes. But freedom isn't necessarily always a good thing.'

Hannah Booth.
'Good Company,'
Design Week
3 (23 September, 2004).

The argument most frequently given against working in-house is that the designer is required to work on the same narrow range of projects. This can often be true, but it is not always the case. And besides, in the early stages of your career, there's not much harm in working doggedly at the same task over and over again. It enables you to develop your working procedures and teaches you numerous valuable lessons. Working in-house may sometimes lack the fizz and glamor of life in an independent studio, where working without a metaphorical safety net can be stimulating, but as a first step in a career it is rarely a wrong move.

It is only by meeting people in both environments that you will gain sufficient insight to allow you to decide which is best for you. In fact, here's another little nostrum to add to the list that we're accumulating: there's no such thing as a bad interview. Even the bad ones are good; I learned a lot about design and life from being interviewed by idiots. At the very least it taught me how to treat interview candidates when, years later, I had to interview designers myself. But it also taught me how each employer looks for something different, and how important human relationships are in the process of finding a job. I recommend attending as many interviews as you can – even unpromising ones (you can always say no if offered a job) – in order to weigh up the pluses and minuses of life in-house against life in the independent sector, and to acquire valuable interview skills.

Working for an independent design studio

Design studios are a mixture of slave camp and enchanted playground; the good ones maintain a balance between these two polarities. You can't avoid the slave camp resemblance – you will have to work long hours with not much pay and little recognition. But you won't mind this, because among all the relentless pressure you will glimpse moments of enchantment. You will see the pleasure that comes from doing good work and making a contribution (singly or collaboratively) to the studio's output. And there's the camaraderie of being with like-minded people. Studio life is often as good as working life gets. [4]

There are, naturally, disappointments, personal rebuffs and collective failures to be found in studio life. But always remember, there are millions of people who'd swap jobs with you if they could. Stop anyone in the street and ask them what sort of work they'd like to do, and most will reply: 'something creative.' In our post-industrial world, no-one wants to do unrewarding work. We all want the buzz of 'making a contribution.' As designers, we are privileged, we get to make something, and get paid for having smart ideas that affect the lives of, perhaps, millions of our fellow citizens. And remembering this makes the knock-backs easier to take, and it makes it easier to live with the fact that we'll always earn less than stockbrokers.

4   In his profile of Bruce Mau, in *Fast Company* (October 2000), Scott Kirsner creates a beguiling snapshot of studio life: 'Inside the high-ceilinged loft space on the edge of Toronto's Chinatown are tall metal bookshelves, drafting tables, digital-video editing suites, architectural models, and scores of hard-working professionals. The deadline pressure is palpable, and couriers make breathless entrances and exits throughout the afternoon. Even as 6 p.m. approaches, not one employee makes a move to head for home. Instead, everyone on staff clusters around a tray of fresh fruit brought in by Cathy Jonasson, the firm's vice president and managing director.'

Apprenticeship

It's an unfashionable word with connotations of servility and poverty, but no matter what you call it, serving an apprenticeship is a necessary and unavoidable step on the road to becoming a mature designer. And it needn't be a dispiriting experience. The energizing charge that comes from learning from more experienced designers is invigorating. In design school you are thrown in with others in the same predicament as yourself. Everyone is similarly aged, and everyone is engaged in the struggle to find a voice and a foothold on the design career path, and everyone is working, for the most part, in the hypothetical realm. But, when you start work, the hypothetical becomes the actual, and you are suddenly working alongside people who may be well advanced along the career path, and who may be sophisticated and articulate designers who have found their own voice. This can be intimidating. Some young designers never get over the shock of working next to experienced designers and retreat into self-doubt and feelings of inadequacy. It's a decisive moment in a designer's education: how you deal with it shapes your future. Happily, most find contact with experienced designers inspirational, and it provides a timely impetus for personal development.

Working alongside an experienced designer will teach you more than almost anything else, especially if the designer is a generous and helpful individual – and you can be cheered by the fact that most designers *are* generous and helpful. This is the moment when you realize that there are huge gaps in your knowledge; that you don't know how to organize your work; that your typography is unexpectedly raw and crude; that you are tongue-tied with clients, and briefs seem painfully limiting. It is the moment when you decide that you are really not as good as you thought you were.

Some designers, when they reach this realization, erect a protective shell to try and obscure the fact that they are deficient in certain areas. This is dangerous. It is much better to ask for help. Few designers, even when up against punishing deadlines, will refrain from helping a new designer. You must ask for help: you are serving an apprenticeship, but it is a modern apprenticeship, and you will have to be prepared to make a nuisance of yourself if you are to be heard. You will have to show willingness and boundless enthusiasm and you will have to show that you want to learn.

Armin Vit writes: 'As junior designers – the common launching pad for designers – we are expected to pay our dues by working long hours on thankless work that in our view poses no real professional challenge, while learning the ropes in the shadows of Senior Designers, Creative Directors and Principals. It has worked for decades … but if we are lucky enough to land a job with a prominent designer we can call it an apprenticeship and look back fondly on the experience'.
'The Young and Not So Restless', *Voice: AIGA Journal of Design*
5 (4 June, 2004).

Some recruitment agencies are said to be good. My philosophy as an employer of design talent has always been to find talent by my own efforts. The act of looking (attending degree shows, visiting colleges, etc.) is a rewarding and informative exercise in itself. Furthermore, I've always believed that there is something lacking in a
6 design company that can't attract a steady flow of talent to its doorstep.

Finding a job in a design studio

Before you can land a job, you need to know where to look for jobs. A lucky few get picked on the strength of their portfolio reviews, or by impressing a visiting designer invited to lecture at the student's college. But for most, it's a matter of looking for vacancies. There are a number of ways of finding out who is hiring. Look in the design press, trawl the internet and ask around. You might also consider signing up with a recruitment agency that finds personnel for studios.

In fact, many hirings are made by studio heads ring-ing acquaintances and asking them if they've seen any hot talent. I've been asked this question many times by friends looking for designers. It means that it's never a waste of time showing your portfolio to anyone who will look at it – because who knows, you may not get a job offer, but ten minutes after your interview, your interviewer might get a call from someone asking if they've seen anyone good.[7]

The most likely route to finding a job is by the sweat of your brow, and you need to approach studios regardless of whether they are recruiting or not. You can start by drawing up a list of your favorites. Remember, however, that your favorites are probably everyone else's favorites. So be wary of approaching only the cool, hip studios, or the better known ones. They get lots of approaches from good people, so be clever and look into the less well-illuminated corners of the design world.

For many young designers, the way into full-time employment is through internships. A successful spell as an intern can often lead to job offers. I've employed many designers this way. If I'm not sure about someone, an internship is a low-risk way of testing them. The designer given an internship must firstly use this as an opportunity to learn – but also as an unrivalled opportunity to impress. Look for ways of making yourself indispensable.

If it's a small studio, answer the phone if you hear it ringing, and take an accurate mes-sage; offer to get sandwiches at lunch time for overworked colleagues. Always turn up on time, and don't rush out of the door as soon as the day is over. Design is about commitment: if you want to have a nine-to-five existence, become a civil servant. We've already noted that the life of a designer is privileged – but there is a price to be paid for this privilege and that price is unflinch-ing commitment. You have to be prepared to make sacrifices.

Approaching a design studio

Never forget, when approaching a studio, that you will be judged by the quality of your approach. Your phone call, your e-mail, your letter will be scrutinized like a sniffer dog checks for contraband at an airline luggage carousel; get it right and you're halfway there, get it wrong and the prospect of stacking super-market shelves starts to beckon. You'd be amazed how many people make a hash of their initial approach. I've received handwritten letters on ruled paper ripped from a spiral-bound notebook. I've received letters where the designer hasn't both-ered to design his or her own letterhead. I've received letters in which the writer couldn't even be bothered to spell my name correctly.[8] And most heinous of all, I've received letters which began Dear Sir or Madam. I throw away anything that begins Dear Sir or Madam. It tells me everything I need to know about the individual who wrote the letter – it tells me that the writer

[7]   An hour or so after writing these words I was called by a designer friend and asked if I'd seen anyone good recently. You see, it happens all the time!

[8]   This is not vanity. My name is not easy to spell. But if an applicant can't be bothered to get it right, it suggests they might be slapdash or lazy in other matters of detail – an unacceptable failing in a graphic designer.

couldn't be bothered to discover the correct spelling of my hard-to-spell name, and it also tells me that I needn't take this any further.

It's easy to get this stuff right. You decide what method of approach you want to use – a letter, phone call or e-mail – and you do it properly. Think of it as your first professional job – selling yourself. Not many designers are taught how to do this in design school, so you will have to learn to do it yourself. But it's not difficult.

I favor the old-fashioned letter. It is the least intrusive method of approach, and it allows you to meticulously prepare your proposal. Even more importantly, a letter is an elemental form of graphic communication. It is a good test of your abilities to formulate a message. Do it well, and you will benefit: do it badly and you will reduce greatly your chances of finding a job.

First, you must have a letterhead. It needn't be foil-blocked with eighteen Pantone colors. A simple black and white DTP document will do – but sweat blood over it to make it visually arresting and professionally functioning. Letterheads are part of the DNA of graphic design. You're not much of a graphic designer unless you've designed a successful letterhead, and the rise of e-mail hasn't made them any less important. And when you are designing a letterhead, always design it with the letter's text on the page. It's a common mistake, but designers usually create letterheads leaving the text area clear. This looks cool, and designerish, but a letterhead is made to be written on, and the recipient of a letter will never see the blank version.

Once you've targeted a studio (or, better yet, studios) you need to find out who is responsible for recruiting. This will necessitate research, and almost certainly a phone call to get the name (and spelling) of the person you need to write to. When you're making the call it's worth remembering that if the company is of a certain size it will have a receptionist. Receptionists are important people in design companies. They often double up as administrators and they are usually influential figures with a finely developed sense of who should have access to their employers. As a general rule, it is worth being polite to receptionists (as a general rule it is worth being polite to everyone), but it is doubly so in the case of design company receptionists. They are a powerful breed with good instincts about who will 'fit in' and who won't.

Having found the name of the person responsible for recruiting, a good letter is now required. The rules are simple. Make your letter short (one sheet only). Make it literate, sharp and to the point: say who you are, what you do and what you want. Nothing else. Well, there is one other thing you could add: a line or two of mild flattery. State that you are aware of Studio X's marvellous work for Client X, and that you have found it inspirational. Don't lay it on too thick, but designers are vain and will respond with Pavlovian slavering to a bit of mild, but honest, praise. It also has the added benefit of demonstrating that you know something about the work of the company that you are applying to.

Request an interview, not a job. If there are no vacancies (highly likely) it is easy for an employer to brush you off with 'Sorry, no vacancies.' It is much less easy to refuse a request for an interview. (You can perhaps help by stating that you are aware that there may be no vacancies, but that you'd value the opportunity to meet and have a judgment on your portfolio.) Most designers are kind-hearted, sympathetic characters who have traveled the same path as you, and will, with a bit of friendly cajoling, agree to a portfolio review. Exploit the innate kindness of designers.

Next, you need to include some samples of work. If you are a moving-image designer, a web designer or a multimedia designer, you might feel the need to include DVDs, CD-ROMs and video cassettes. Try and resist this urge. Instead, add a few sheets of paper showing stills or frames from your work laid out in a clear and precise manner. Designers in busy studios (and you should assume that they are all busy – if they are not, they definitely won't be hiring) rarely have time to stop and look at discs and tapes; it is just too time consuming. Much better to give them something to provoke an instant response and prompt them to offer to see you. If they agree to see you, then you can show discs or tapes. Sending an e-mail with a link to a website is acceptable.

If you are job hunting in a period when design is in the economic doldrums (roughly every ten years, in my experience), then you might have to write so many letters and attend so many fruitless interviews that you begin to wonder about the wisdom of becoming a designer. But persistence, doggedness and barefaced cheek will pay off.[9]

The worst thing that can happen is that you become disheartened. If your search for a job is going badly, you must urgently reassess. You must search for ways of refining your presentation. Try tweaking your letter and changing the work samples you're sending. If they are not getting a response, perhaps they're not as sharp or as effective as you think they are. You might also be targeting the wrong people, so rethink your list of potential employers. Reassessment and rigorous self-appraisal are the keys to being a good designer.

It's also worth considering doing things that attract attention and bring potential employers to you. In the 1960s, the wonderful Italian designer Germano Facetti decorated the ceiling of a friend's book shop in London. It was seen by the founder of Penguin, Allen Lane, who appointed Facetti to restyle the Penguin imprint – for which he has become justly famous. You might, however, choose to avoid the ruse used by the designer who sent a box of live locusts to the creative director of a well-known British advertising agency, in an attempt to get noticed. The creative director invited the young hopeful to an interview, where he revealed himself to be an ardent animal-lover and proceeded to berate the unfortunate interviewee for his cruelty to living creatures.

[9] I don't, however, recommend that you turn up unannounced at studios. Although I once had a young designer turn up and demand that I interview him: I was impressed with his chutzpah, so I agreed. I ended up offering him a job on the spot – but he was a sort of genius.

The interview

If you get your approach right, you will be invited to interview. Look at each interview as a substantial victory. Think about what you've achieved by getting an interview: you've persuaded a busy creative director, senior designer or studio head to stop what they are doing and give you their time and attention. Congratulations. You should be pleased.

In interviews, your character is under as much scrutiny as your work. How you conduct yourself is as important as the work you show. You can begin by being on time, and being friendly and considerate. If this sounds obvious to you, I apologize, but I've come across many candidates who don't think these details are the least bit important. Don't assume, either, that you have unlimited time. Your interviewer may specify a time limit, but make sure your presentation can be delivered in under fifteen minutes (this includes small talk and admiring comments about the studio's tasteful brochure you picked up in reception).

I am now going to say something that is so obvious you will be tempted to stop reading this book and throw it away, but don't. Even if this is a crime you are not guilty of, pass the information on to others because there are many offenders; I should know, I've interviewed dozens of designers who've committed this monstrous offence. What am I talking about? Spitting at the interviewer? Calling into doubt the interviewer's personal hygiene? No, worse. I'm talking about designers who show their portfolios to themselves. I used to keep quiet about this. When a designer sat down in front of me and showed me half of their portfolio, while they viewed the other half, I'd remain silent and crane my neck. Now I say, in my best school teacher voice: 'Excuse me, who are you showing your portfolio to?' This is usually met with bewilderment, and it's only when I grab the portfolio and turn it to face me, that the realization of what they are doing sinks in. So here's the rule: when showing a portfolio, turn it to face the interviewer. If your work is on a laptop, then do the same with the laptop – position the screen directly in front of the interviewer (it is perfectly acceptable to plonk yourself next to your interviewer so that you can operate the machine). I told you it was simple, but you'd be astonished by how many designers don't bother to turn their work to face the person, or persons, they are showing it to. 10 Interviewing someone who does this is a bit like going to a gig and having a pillar in front of you. The first law of presentation is let your interviewer see the show.

During the interview, talk succinctly about your work. Avoid excessive detail and allow the interviewer to ask questions. An interviewer who doesn't ask questions is probably not interested in your work. Be alert to the microclimate of the interview; signs of inattentiveness and distraction in the interviewer mean that you are not getting through. Either your work, or your personality, is not captivating him or her, so you must alter your approach. The most likely cause is that you are giving too much information. Your interviewer will be capable of assessing your work without long rambling descriptions, so only give enough information to support what the viewer can see for him- or herself. Go through it quickly, but don't rush it, and allow the interviewer to dictate the pace. Be passionate and proud of your work, show that you care deeply about what you do, but also show that you are not complacent and that you strive for improvement.

Once you have shown your work, wait for the interviewer to comment. If you are lucky, you will get an instant verdict. Even if the verdict is unfavorable, you are being given valuable information, so use it to realign your approach in readiness for the next interview. If the verdict is favorable, the conversation might be drawn towards money. Well-run studios will have a policy on what they pay interns or junior designers. It's rarely a large sum, so don't start planning a spending spree, but whatever you do, do not offer to work for nothing. Any studio that doesn't pay its interns is not worth working for (these are the same studios that moan about clients demanding unpaid pitches). You may choose to ignore this piece of advice, but after working for a few weeks without pay you'll see what I mean. I mentioned earlier that all jobs are good ones. I should have said that all jobs *that offer remuneration* are good jobs.

If you've made a big splash and your interviewer is interested in you, then you might be asked what sort of salary you want. Tread carefully, this question means that the studio has no policy on salaries. Don't be drawn on this. Say that you need enough money to live on, and that you are open to reasonable offers, and leave it at that. Most studios know what they can afford, and are only trying to get you on the cheap.

If you are offered a job on the spot – it happens – you've done well. You should ask for written confirmation (a good studio will do this anyway) and you can now go celebrate. A more likely scenario is that the interviewer will request that you 'keep in touch'. This is also a good sign. It shows that you have made a mark, but most importantly it gives you a 'contact'. In other words, here is someone who you can legitimately approach again in a few months' time. After a dozen good interviews you may not have any job offers, but you will have accumulated a great address book. Everyone you see becomes a contact.

The follow-up

After every interview you need to leave something behind. Ideally something small, striking and easily stored. A postcard with contact details pinned to a sheet of paper showing two or three of your best pieces of work will do. Or you can be adventurous and produce something innovative – a handmade (or printed) booklet, for example. At the end of one interview I conducted with a young designer, I was given a poster, covered in a tangle of graphic equations and symbols. It was a complex graph charting his attempts to find work, and listed every designer and studio he'd approached (including some famous names). The poster carried verbatim telephone conversations and reproduced e-mails (including one of my own), few of which showed the senders in a good light. I was impressed with his audacity and graphic diligence, but I also couldn't help but be a tiny bit offended by seeing my private e-mail reproduced. He didn't get the job, which is not to say he wasn't good.

The task of promoting yourself to your newly acquired network of contacts is critical. You mustn't be over-zealous; you need to be sparing but effective. E-mails or letters are best – although phone calls can also work now, since your target knows who you are, and will be less reluctant to talk to you than before. Here you will see the benefits of cultivating relationships with studio receptionists. But don't become a pest. It's a fine line between being a nuisance and keeping prospective employers informed about your activities.

Consider designing some sort of mailer. It should be something striking and confident and show that you have made progress since your previous interview. To achieve this you may need to create some self-initiated projects to keep it stoked with new work. Design letterheads for friends, websites for unsigned bands, do anything to keep your hand in and to expand your portfolio.

Personal portfolios

Your portfolio is your shop window. It doesn't matter whether it is a printed portfolio or a laptop presentation, the same rules apply: make it as compelling and as revealing as possible. Push yourself. Don't think, oh this will do. It won't. After your personality, it is the second most valuable tool that you possess to help you find a job.

A portfolio of eight to ten interesting pieces of work is ideal. Any more and you risk dragging out the interview. Avoid duplication; if you have two similar projects, be ruthless and only show one. Ideally your work should be printed out as high quality, ink-jet, color outputs. The advantage of this is that it is cheap, and allows frequent updates. Make sure your printouts are of the highest quality. They should be loose individual sheets, which allow the interviewer to hold them and look at them freely. Loose sheets, covered in replaceable acetate, are preferable to sheets clipped together in a ring binder (attaching them and detaching them can be distracting). [11] Each page is a mini portfolio. It can show the finished job, or it can show developmental work. I wouldn't recommend anything too large. There is something off-putting about a huge portfolio – plus it's a health hazard if you are out on a windy day.

11 A designer friend of mine recently told me that he wouldn't consider a designer for a position in his studio – no matter how talented – if his work was presented in a portfolio with ring-binder clips. 'I'd sooner take on someone with a forked tail and horns,' he said.

Your portfolio sheets should exhibit a degree of uniformity. Create a grid, and make sure every project adheres to the grid. This will be difficult because you might be showing a variety of projects (2D and 3D), but it's worth trying to get this right because you will be judged on how your work is presented as much as by the work itself. A portfolio that has an underlying unity and structure will score more points (and be more enjoyable to view) than one that has no structure or cohesion.

Print designers will naturally want to show finished specimens – printed books, brochures, letterheads, etc. Hand these items over to the interviewer immediately, and don't flick through them admiringly as if you were seeing them for the first time – people do, I promise you.

I'd avoid sketchbooks. To seasoned employers, they all tend to look the same; it is like new parents showing you a picture of their baby: enchanting to them, less so to those without biological ties to the adored infant. However, I'm sure there are employers who like to look at sketchbooks, so if you have one that you are especially proud of, bring it along, but I suggest that you only show it if asked. Working drawings are more useful. Some designers place great importance on them. But not every item of work needs to be accompanied by working drawings. Two or three at most will suffice, and only if they show clear developmental thinking.

What sort of physical portfolio should you have? A bag or box that is easy to open, that allows your work to be viewed easily and which protects the work as you scurry from interview to interview. Keep your portfolio clean. It should not look as if it lives in a mildewed cellar when not being used. No employer will expect a custom-made flight-case designed by Philippe Starck, but valuable points can be won for a distinctive case or carrier. Remember, your interviewer has probably had years of looking at identical slim black portfolio bags, so a nicely designed, unostentatious box will strike a refreshing note.

One last thing: mark your portfolio in some way so that when you open it, it is ready for viewing. It can be distracting to see a portfolio opened upside down, and have to wait while it is turned over. It's a tiny detail, but your success might depend on tiny details. We'll talk more about portfolios when we get to the subject of studio portfolios (where the approach is different).

What do employers really want?

Ask a hundred employers this question and you will get a hundred different answers, but my guess is that they are all looking for someone they get on with. In the intimate and psychologically revealing space of a design studio, we have to 'get on' with the people we work with. Keep this in mind when you are being interviewed. Look for ways to reassure a prospective employer that you are hard-working, adaptable and socially well adjusted. No need to rattle on about your talent – an experienced designer will be able to assess your merits as a designer within a few seconds of opening your portfolio. Assessing your personality is harder – the least you can do is help. Stress that you don't mind doing the dreary stuff and that you are happy to assist senior designers; show a willingness to understand the studio's culture; show that you already know something about the studio's work; and most importantly, trust your personality, and trust your work.

Hiring a graduate – or a junior designer – is not a risk-free undertaking. Try to think about your suitability from the employer's point of view. What are the risks they are assessing? The risk for an employer is mainly financial: even a low salary can put a strain on a small studio. There will be other considerations. Will the new individual require lots of attention? Will the new person fit into the studio culture? Yet the most common concern when assessing a new recruit is calculating how long it will take for this new individual to reach effectiveness. The six to eighteen months that I estimate as the time it might take for a graduate to become effective is a perilously long time for a small employer to wait.

Approaching an in-house studio

All the above applies equally to finding a job within a business that operates an in-house studio, with the possible exception that you might be interviewed by a non-designer; for example, it might be a marketing manager or a communications manager or the head of the company. Being interviewed by a non-designer requires a slightly different approach. Your interviewer will almost certainly have some knowledge of design – but it might be a rather self-centered interest and stretch no further than his or her own company or products. You will have to compensate for this by using plain language and avoiding design-oriented exposition. You don't have to compromise – you simply have to make an allowance for the fact that your interviewer is not a designer.

In conclusion I'd say: learn to enjoy interviews. View them as precious opportunities to study the thinking and working process of designers and studios; as an opportunities to have your work critiqued by your peers; as ways of measuring your progress. Don't be afraid to ask for a blunt assessment of your work, and if the comments seem valid and worthwhile, act on them quickly.

At some time in the future, you will perhaps interview designers yourself, and you will look back on the ordeal of being interviewed with a different perspective. You might also have occasion to have your early attempts to recruit designers come back to confront you. I was recently introduced to the designer Fred Deakin – a partner in the London-based Airside, and a member of Lemon Jelly. He told me that I had – many years before – interviewed him. I tensed. I didn't remember the interview (which doesn't say much for my talent-spotting powers). I asked him if the interview had gone well; 'Yes,' he said. 'You were very helpful.' I was relieved.

Natalie Hunter

After graduating from Edinburgh University, where she studied Human-Computer Interface Psychology, Nat worked in Edinburgh as a graphic designer in the music industry. In 1993, she continued her studies at the Royal College of Art, embarking on the country's first master's program in Interactive Multimedia. After graduation, she worked freelance for several years and became involved in creating special effects for the movie *Lost In Space,* producing CD-ROMs and designing interactive performances and installations. In 1999, with Alex Maclean and Fred Deakin, she started the highly regarded design company Airside, perhaps best known for its work for Lemon Jelly (of which Fred Deakin is a member). They have a diverse range of clients, including the BBC, Carhartt, Channel 4, Greenpeace, the Hayward Gallery, London Underground, Médecins du Monde, MTV Europe, The Royal College of Art, the Serpentine Gallery, VW Radio and White Cube Gallery.

www.airside.co.uk

Dot Com Refugees · Plastic figures shown with packaging

Designed
by Airside

AS What did you learn at design school that helps you today? NH I didn't go to design school first time round – I studied psychology. The part of the program that completely inspired me was the Human-Computer Interface module. It was all about how computers were being used to change people's interactions with other people in situations like post-stroke patients or kids who were failing at school. I realized how dynamics could be set up between people and machines that were completely invaluable, and I was hooked. I then learned how to program computers at a bank, but it was a miserable environment so I managed to get myself a job at a small graphic design company: initially doing the accounts, but soon I became junior designer and was trained up on the job in design, typography and use of the process camera (!). It was all music industry work and I loved it. A few years later, the company went bust and I went to the RCA to do an MA in Interactive Multimedia. It was a funny old program, but I learned how to work effectively in a team, and that a successful piece of work is often not as much about the content as the way you present it.

What prompted you to set up Airside? Freelance work was exciting and plentiful, but it was erratic and it was rare to be involved in the creative process from the start. I wanted to create an environment where I worked with people I liked and respected, where we could have fun and play with ideas.

What were the biggest problems that faced you in the early stages? Managing our workload was tough, and worrying about where the next client was going to come from. Also, employing people for the first time was a real eye-opener – our personnel skills had to be honed very fast.

Airside are famous for their cross-media approach to design – does this versatility bring any problems? People tend to only know us for one thing – T-shirts, illustration, websites or animation. They are often really surprised when they realize what other areas we work in.

Airside has a strong stylistic identity, which attracts many people, but does it ever work against you? We don't intend to have a strong stylistic identity at all. We are very ideas-led. We always start with an idea, and the implementation then follows. Sometimes we do work that doesn't look like people's preconceptions of us, and sometimes we do work that does – it just depends how the process goes. The most annoying thing is when people ask for a job to be carried out in a particular style, usually one that we're trying desperately to move on from.

How does Airside find clients? We've mostly found work through word of mouth. Occasionally we make trips to ad agencies and show them our portfolio, but usually we respond to people phoning and asking for our portfolio. We're beginning to be more proactive rather than reactive now, as it would be better for us to have more control over the sort of clients we work for.

Airside is unusual in that it has a website that sells its own products and makes additional income for the company. Is this a viable route for others to follow? Yes, I think that any design company could do this, and many do. It's a useful means of self-expression within the company, allowing employees to do non-client-based work. It's also useful research for us to have direct retail contact with a market that we are often asked to design for by clients.

What is your philosophy or company ethos? Treat everyone as you would like to be treated. Have as much fun as you possibly can whilst working. Communicate with everyone honestly and openly.

What do you do to cultivate a good company profile? Do our best work for the people we want to work for. I don't think we consciously cultivate anything, but our choice of clients speaks volumes about us. The work we've done for Lemon Jelly is probably the single most useful way we've cultivated our company profile.

What is your long-term vision for your company? More work in Japan, higher turnover, more profit, small growth to fifteen people and perhaps satellite offices abroad, since Airsiders get itchy feet!

Designed
by Airside

The US Department of Labor report cited in the introduction to this book states that out of more than 500,000 designers (graphic, industrial, interior, etc.) nearly one-third were 'self-employed – almost five times the proportion for all professionals and related occupations.' The report goes on to say: 'Keen competition is expected for most jobs, despite average projected employment growth, because many talented individuals are attracted to careers as designers.'

It's official then: the design world is tough and competitive. And just to make matters worse, the design schools annually deposit thousands of students into the job market with the result that there are simply not enough jobs to go round. So why make it any tougher on yourself by setting up on your own as a self-employed freelance designer, with its attendant risks and uncertainties? For some, it is a matter of personal choice; they find that they are temperamentally suited to the freelance life. For others, the freelance existence is, increasingly, the only option.

Design is either a solitary or a communal activity depending on your aesthetic view and psychological make-up. However, I'm surprised by how often the attraction of 'working collaboratively' is cited by designers as a desirable goal. It is often mentioned by designers as the most rewarding aspect of design, more important even than the end result. Nor is this a view expressed only by young designers looking for the emotional and practical support that comes from working in a group. It is often expressed by experienced designers, who relish the creative chain reaction set in motion by the collaborative process. However, there are individuals who relish the solitary approach to design, and for these individuals, setting up in freelance practice and working alone is a creative necessity.

In my experience, the freelance life suits two types of designers. The first type is the very able and resourceful individual with specialist skills – Photoshop wizard, skilled typographer, the After Effects specialist, Flash animator, etc. They can charge handsomely for their services, knowing that when their task is finished they are free to move on, or free to have a week at home doing as they please. Initially they may struggle to acquire a sustainable flow of work, but over time these individuals build up a client base that results in regular commissions.

The second type is best characterized as the creative loner. These are individuals with a strong personal vision that cannot be comfortably accommodated within the structure of a design group or an in-house studio. They are often designers who cannot compromise their work. The Norwegian designer Kim Hiorthøy exemplifies all the best qualities of a freelance, independent-minded designer. He works alone because: 'I've always done it and I'm comfortable with it.' I asked him in an e-mail conversation to describe the advantages and disadvantages of the freelance life: 'I very often change things completely at whim,' he states, 'and often at the very end of working on something. Not having to explain or argue is an advantage, I think. I know that could sound like a disadvantage as well, but so far it's often felt like it was for the better.'

Courtesy of Kim Hiorthøy

Design by
Kim Hiorthøy

Even if you don't fit into either of the categories described above, you may still be attracted to freelance life, but setting up as a freelance designer straight from design school requires an abundance of stamina, personal confidence and business savvy. For most, it is better to do a couple of years within a studio before setting out as a self-employed designer: having experienced life in a well-run studio, you will be better equipped to deal with the precariousness of freelance life.

For freelance designers an increasingly viable option is to rent studio space with other like-minded freelance designers. This allows you to retain creative and fiscal control over your life, but at the same time allows you to exchange ideas and share resources. It is also possible to take advantage of the increasing trend among big and small studios to hire freelance talent. Studios have always done this, but in difficult times, when business is slow, bringing talent in only when it is needed has become commonplace. For the young freelance designer this is a good alternative to going solo. It allows you to sample studio life, gives you an insight into how different studios function and provides you with a pool of contacts that you can call on again and again.

If you get it right – if you are psychologically suited to the life – a freelance existence can be creatively rewarding and financially beneficial. If you've got good clients who pay you adequately, and on time, then the financial benefits from being self-employed are considerable. Financial advisers and tax experts will tell you that it is the most financially advantageous situation to be in: with careful planning and meticulous administration you can maximize the benefits of being self-employed.

You may be able to work from home – in a garage, a loft or a spare room, but this only suits certain individuals. Many people find the prospect of being at home all day, every day, unappealing: the prospect of your own company for long uninterrupted spells can be dispiriting. But for others, working from home is highly desirable: no studio rent to pay and no tiring commute every day. You need to be sure that clients can visit you easily and you need to think about what your address says about you: does an obviously domestic address make you look cheap and flaky? With fast internet connections, cellular phones and inexpensive courier services it is increasingly feasible to be based anywhere in the world. So why not at home?

Perhaps the single most important aspect of being self-employed is that you retain flexibility: by staying small (you can't get any smaller than being solo) you are free to turn work down and free to do only the work you want to do. The pressure to take on unappealing assignments is much less when you only have yourself to feed. The English designer Michael C. Place worked for Designers Republic for nearly a decade, but he left to set up Build, a one-man studio based in London. As he explains: 'It was something I had been planning to do for a while, and it just seemed the right thing to do. Working for someone else wasn't an option that I had considered. I've come to value the satisfaction of getting work on

In an interview in *Eye* (Summer 2000), designer Lorraine Wild noted the charms of garage working: 'There's something very comfortable and productive about the garage. Being there has as much to do with adjusting to the realities of being a parent of a very young child as it does to the analysis of what is – and isn't – necessary for the production of interesting work. It is somewhat of an anti-office in that it is not about giving oneself over entirely to maintaining the contemporary corporate standard of design production. The space is configured to the work that I want to do. Perhaps it has to do with my upbringing in Detroit, where garages are often the site of great creativity (both automotive and musical), or the influence of my teacher Paul Rand, who worked out of his kitchen for years.'

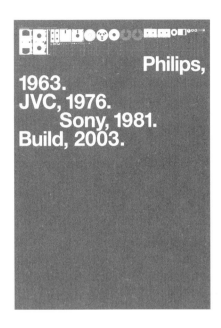

Poster and magazine
by Build

my own merit, and by my own hard work, rather than the fact I worked at a well-known agency. It means a lot to me that Build is my own thing and that I have built it up from nothing.'

I've already mentioned the drawback of not having other designers to exchange ideas with. On a stolidly practical note, working in a studio means that when you encounter one of those knotty software problems that all designers face, you can wander over to the next desk and get an instant answer. On your own, you might have to look it up in the manual – and we know how torturous that can be (who designs those things?).

You will have to be prepared to do your own finances – tax planning, invoicing, cash flow control, debt chasing and banking. In her book *The Professional Practice of Design,* Dorothy Goslett notes: 'Many designers, though admitting its necessity, think that design administration is boring, a tiresome chore always to be put aside for doing second if something more exciting crops up to be done first. But good design + good administration = good fees well-earned.' Goslett's equation (first written in 1960) may discourage certain individuals, but it is unavoidably true. It is widely assumed that designers are not very good at administration. This is often the case, but by no means universal. Good administration skills can be acquired and become habitual.

Finding work when you are on your own is tough. A printer friend once told me that if you only start looking for work when you need to, then it's too late. What he meant was that you need to be looking for work even when you are busy. Easy to say, and easy to do if you are a big studio with lots of people – but on your own, it becomes an onerous chore. As Goslett notes: 'This [finding clients] will be the main battle of your whole freelance career: not only to find clients to start you going but constantly to be finding clients to keep you going. It is a battle which has to be waged more or less ceaselessly until you retire and one which will never allow you to rest on your laurels.'

Are you disciplined enough to work on your own? In most studios, there's a healthy sense of communal activity that motivates almost by contagion – you can't sit about doing nothing when everyone else is working like demons. As Michael Place notes: 'I sometimes miss the fact that you can't just ask someone what they think of a piece of work, but I now have a network of people that I can e-mail and get an opinion or a critique. I also miss the banter. But this is compensated for in other ways; I tend to work long hours and so having the studio at home means I can concentrate on my work without the hassle of a commute.'

On your own, you have to be more disciplined, not less. You have to make your own schedules. You have to resist the allure of the fridge and daytime television (actually, if you can't resist daytime television you should consider a career change). Also, the act of leaving the house every day to go to a place of work, and being out in the world is good for creativity – street posters, architecture, favorite shops, faces in the crowd, galleries, book shops, going to the sandwich shop at lunchtime – all contribute to the building of an alert design sensibility. Even the ugly stuff – the crass billboards and the trashy magazines on news-stands – informs the way we think about our work.

The salaried employee gets a paycheck every month – the freelance employee has to send out invoices and wait for clients to pay. Then there is the perennial problem of late payment. Since freelancers are unlikely to threaten a corporation that is a slow payer – why risk losing a source of work by being aggressive? – no firm is going to worry unduly about making a freelancer wait for his or her money. This puts a strain on cash flow (and nerves) and is the cause of most non-creative problems for the self-employed designer. Spending time chasing up outstanding debts is a vital if unenjoyable activity for the freelance designer. [2]

If you are setting up in freelance practice, you will need to buy equipment, software, furniture and materials. All this requires a degree of financial planning that you will perhaps need help with. You will also need to know how to cost projects and how to charge. These more practical issues are dealt with in the chapter devoted to running a studio.

[2] In the modern business world, aggressive behavior is often thought to be necessary. If a payment is late, you are supposed to yell at someone. My advice is to do the opposite. Approach the individuals concerned with the utmost politeness; make friends with your clients' finance departments, they are rarely the villains. When you get a check in the post, call and thank them. Designers like to have their work praised, and so too do clerks in accounting offices.

Clients

What sort of clients use freelance designers? Clients are attracted to freelance designers for the same three reasons that clients are attracted to studios or design firms:

1   Creative reasons – *Does this person do the sort of work I want?*
2   Financial reasons – *Freelancers are cheaper than big studios.*
3   Personal reasons – *Do I get along with this person?*

A client may have a personal preference for working with individuals rather than big studios with their account handlers and project managers. You might add other factors like convenience or speciality, and it is essential when setting yourself up as a freelancer that you have reasons for clients to come to you: you need factor X.

Factor X is usually personal. The personal always plays a part in any designer/client relationship – never underestimate it. Clients invariably work with people they like. I once got a call from a guy who ran a medium-sized business: each year he commissioned a substantial amount of graphic design. I was invited to go and see him. He explained that he'd been working with a talented designer for the past year or so, but that the relationship had gone sour. 'His work is great' he explained, 'but I'm fed up with him moaning all the time.' It appeared that the designer had made the relationship unpleasant, and as result, he'd lost the client. The client had no gripe with the designer's work, he just didn't like the designer's attitude.

If 'personal reasons' and 'creative reasons' are self-explanatory (a client has to like you *and* your work), 'financial reasons' is less easy to gauge. In the eyes of many clients, a freelance designer will be a less expensive option than hiring a studio with its heftier overheads. The freelancer can use this to his or her advantage. By stressing that you offer all the skills and creativity of a bigger studio but at a lower cost, you can sometimes steal work away from bigger studios. However, smallness can also work against you; some clients will avoid freelance designers because they prefer the comfort of a studio with a range of dedicated personnel, and are happy to pay the higher fees involved.

The ability to attract and maintain clients is perhaps the most basic test you need to pass if you are going to survive as a freelancer. But assuming you can do this – and many designers can – you still have other factors to consider. You must, for instance, consider what to call yourself. Do you use your own name or do you give yourself a studio name? Using your real name has the virtue of proclaiming your freelance status ('Bob Smith' looks and sounds like … well, Bob Smith), but this can be off-putting to some clients. A studio name has the virtue of making you look like a collective or group, and may initially attract interest. There is another, more practical, advantage in having a 'group name,' as Michael Place points out: 'When the time is right, I would like to eventually employ people and by having a studio name I can do this more easily than if the studio carries just my name.'

Starting up as a freelance designer requires courage. Without first having a spell in a studio learning the mechanics of running a business, it will prove a steep and intimidating climb. You need to carefully assess all the relevant factors before embarking on the freelance life, but if you decide that it is right for you then there are some practical decisions to be made. Setting up a freelance practice is, in many ways, similar to starting a company – the only difference is that you are CEO, senior designer, junior designer and office assistant, all in one. In the next two chapters you will find some of the information you need to know to continue. Just make sure your shoulders are big enough to take the pressure.

How to be a graphic designer, without losing your soul

Rudy VanderLans

Rudy VanderLans was born in The Hague, the Netherlands. Originally he wanted to become an illustrator, but enrolled in the graphic design department of the Royal Academy of Fine Art. After an apprenticeship at Wim Crouwel's Total Design studio, VanderLans worked at Vorm Vijf and Tel Design. In 1981, he moved to California to do postgraduate studies at the University of California, Berkeley, where he met type designer Zuzana Licko, whom he later married. In 1983, VanderLans started work at the San Francisco *Chronicle* (he thought he was applying for a job at Chronicle Books). He was hired by the editorial art director to do illustrations, cover designs and graphs. He quickly became disillusioned with the demands of a daily newspaper and sought out other creative outlets. In 1984 Rudy VanderLans co-founded Emigre, a digital-type foundry and publisher of graphic-design-related software and printed materials. *Emigre* magazine, edited by VanderLans, offers an unrivaled critical survey of contemporary design issues. VanderLans is the author of three books about outsider musicians (Captain Beefheart, Van Dyke Parks and Gram Parsons). He lives and works in California.

www.emigre.com

Courtesy of Rudy VanderLans

Design by
Rudy VanderLans

AS You trained in Holland before moving to the United States. It is increasingly common for designers to move away from the country of their birth. What are the advantages? RV After graduating from art school and working as a graphic designer with a number of design studios in Holland I became disappointed with graphic design. It was not at all what I had hoped it would be. Especially, working for clients that I had little affinity with made it very difficult for me to feel connected, let alone motivated. So I moved to California to get away from graphic design for a while and to study photography at Berkeley. What I didn't expect was that California at the time was a very exciting place to be for graphic design. The so-called New Wave with designers like April Greiman was starting to bloom, and CalArts was in the early days of its development as an experimental design hothouse with Jeffery Keedy, Ed Fella and Lorraine Wild teaching there. And Henk Elenga and Rick Vermeulen of Hard Werken were out in Los Angeles. All the misfits of graphic design ended up in California, and then the Macintosh computer was thrown into the mix, and it all exploded. It turned out to be quite an advantageous time for me to move, but it was a total coincidence that I happened to end up in the right place at the right time. On the other hand, since to some extent your work is determined by your surroundings, a change of surroundings can do wonders for your creativity.

When you look back at your education were there aspects that you didn't appreciate at the time, but which you now realize have stood you in good stead? There were certain things I enjoyed less than others, such as the endless hours of calligraphy under the guidance of Gerrit Noordzij. I never in my wildest dreams imagined I'd end up designing type, let alone co-running a type foundry, so these exercises didn't interest me that much. But I've come to realize that everything I was taught during those Noordzij classes formed a solid basis for understanding how type is structured. I never imagined those lessons would become so valuable to me. That's the thing about graphic design; there are so many different directions and possibilities within the profession that you'd better become as versatile as possible because you really never know what you might enjoy doing the most.

You said that you wished you'd been taught theory at school. Emigre, in its new book-like incarnation, is almost totally devoted to theory. How, in your view, does theory help the modern designer? I'm not sure if theory helps me to design, but it sure helps me to think critically about all kinds of issues relating to design. I think that's the main purpose theory serves. You are an example of a designer who is not content with just being a hired hand. You are very modest about it, but there's an entrepreneurial side to you. You are a photographer, a writer, an editor, a publisher and co-owner of a type foundry. This is not the typical career path of a graphic designer. Do you think designers who want to do meaningful work are going to have to be more entrepreneurial in the future? Not necessarily. I think designers can do meaningful work for others as long as they choose to work for meaningful clients.

How does the young designer learn about the business side of graphic design? By taking on as many jobs and clients as possible when you first start out and keeping your eyes and ears open. As a designer working for clients you're often in the unique position to peek behind the scenes and get a sense of how others spend their money and run their businesses. Seeing how others were struggling gave me the courage to start out on my own. But ultimately it was through the school of hard knocks that I learned how to run a business. That, and having a partner, my wife Zuzana, who has a terrific knack for detail and accounting, which is an absolute must. Bean counting is a mayor key to the success of any business.

What I learned from working for others was that there seem to be two kinds of ways to go about running a business; you either delegate everything, which means hiring employees and becoming a manager; or you do as much as you can yourself, which means you control nearly everything you do but your output will be limited by the fact that you'll spend your days doing a lot of other stuff besides design. We actually enjoy the latter, and it has served us very well.

When I go to design schools to talk to students I'm always asked how I stop clients interfering with work. I tell them there's no easy answer. Do you have an answer? Yes, and I think the answer's pretty simple. You have to listen very carefully to what the client wants, and be careful not to approach the project with a preconceived idea of what it should look like. In my own experience, too often I approached a design job wanting to use a certain font or a particular typographic mannerism, simply because it's what I felt comfortable with at the time. But that wasn't always what the client wanted.

Design isn't about squeezing square pegs into round holes. It's often said that as designers we should 'educate' our clients, to make them see how they can benefit from our sense of style and good taste. But I think that we can learn much from our clients as well. It's a two-way street. There's been plenty of projects that I've worked on that I initially hated because I had to compromise my preconceived ideas only to realize later that the end result was better because of the client's suggestions.

Young designers seem obsessed with fame, or at least peer recognition. According to Neville Brody, this is the primary motivation for many young designers. What is your response to this trend? It's only natural to want to be revered by your peers. There's nothing wrong with having that ambition. Plus, fame usually translates into more people wanting to hire your services. So from that point of view fame can be quite helpful. But I would have no idea how you'd go about becoming famous. It's not something you can force to happen. And obsessing over it won't make it any easier.

You place great emphasis on the craft of graphic design in everything you do. But in the media landscape we live in, the message is king; it doesn't matter what the message 'looks like' it only matters that it says it. What do you say to someone who says that there's no point in learning the craft of design any more? I'd say they should consider a career in advertising. That kind of a statement is difficult to understand. Doing graphic design without an interest in the craft is like being a soccer player without knowing the basics of ball control. Everybody can kick a ball around, but without ball control you're not going to be very effective.

I'm a big fan of your three books on musicians and their landscapes. There's something novelistic about the way you track these figures (Captain Beefheart, Van Dyke Parks and Gram Parsons) through the Californian landscape. Is this what the critics call graphic authorship? Yes, I believe that's what they'd call it. But no matter what you'd call it, when you combine writing, photography, type design and graphic design, it places you in no-man's-land. Graphic authorship sounds impressive, but it's not a category that book stores or art galleries know how to accommodate. So I'm just as happy if people refer to my work as graphic design or photography, or even art.

Designed by
Rudy VanderLans

59   *'I want to run my own studio. I like doing tax calculations and eighteen-hour days'*

Setting up a studio

The graphic design studio can be an enlightening and fertile place to work in, with an almost utopian sense of freedom. In its ideal state it is a cultural factory staffed by visionary individuals, where the raw materials are ideas and the end product is creative realization. I know that other types of business can claim to be rewarding and fulfilling – any business that is well run and operated with care and respect for other people will be a good place to work. But I've always selfishly believed that the buzz you get from being part of an efficient and productive design studio is hard to beat. There's something uniquely satisfying about being part of a group of people engaged in the creation of a product in which the individuals can claim total, shared or partial authorship.

My proudest moments at Intro were when visitors – clients, suppliers or friends – looked around and said 'I'd like to work here.' We worked hard at building a culture and an atmosphere; we gave people exceptional amounts of freedom in which to conduct their working lives, and as a result, people were happy and productive. When this was recognized by outsiders, it was, for me, far more gratifying than winning design awards or being written about flatteringly in the design press.

Authorship – individual and collective – is the key to the success of a design company. The satisfaction that comes with 'authorship' is a fundamental requirement of modern life. Many businesses deny their employees this; they seek to reduce the working week to rote; they produce rule books that dictate behavior and attitude. And while this suits some people, for others it is anathema. The good design studio is fuelled by the notion that we all want to do meaningful and creative work for which we can claim authorship. In the post-industrial world we want to use our brains, not our muscles; we want to sweat ideas, not bodily fluids. It also helps that studio life is a communal activity, and in good studios everyone enjoys a sort of equality that is rarely encountered elsewhere.

Perhaps all this sounds rather idealistic? In reality, most design studios are places that are characterized by stress, hard work and long hours, interspersed with occasional moments of mild euphoria brought on by creative achievement. Put like this, it's hard to imagine why anyone would ever want to set up and run a design studio. Yet designers continue to strike out on their own, and they continue to set up studios in a perpetual quest for autonomy. The example of Bibliothèque is typical of many designers who reach a point in their careers when the craving for autonomy becomes a call to action. 'Bibliothèque happened by default,' explains founding partner Mason Wells. 'The decision to start our own business was creative and not financial. The three of us had worked at our previous studios (Jon Jeffrey at Farrow, and Tim Beard and me at North) for about eight years and things were beginning to stagnate. No matter how much creativity you assert, you still have to answer to somebody else. This general frustration at the lack of control became a catalyst to just get on with it. Needless to say our frustrations became a positive energy and the business evolved.'

'Between the three of us,' he continues, 'we had ideas that just didn't fit into the framework of our previous jobs. Now we have control and it's incredibly liberating. We work differently and we don't have to answer to anyone but ourselves. It's a far more organic process, allowing us to control every aspect of the job, every step of the way. A year down the line we have worked on jobs we would never have dreamt about. We have built up an excellent client roster and have attained financial stability beyond our previous jobs. Most importantly though, starting Bibliothèque has rekindled our passion for design.'

A desire for more freedom (which brings with it increased responsibility) is only one of the reasons why designers set up studios. Designers start studios and set up companies for many reasons. They do it because they reach an age when an inner voice tells them to take control of their financial destinies; when they realize they don't want to spend the rest of their lives working for someone else; when disenchantment with existing employers arises; when they think they can do it better than the idiot who currently employs them; when a client appears, or circumstances arise, which makes setting up a studio feasible; or when they meet someone in whom they recognize a kindred spirit with whom to set up in practice. And this neatly brings us to the first golden rule of forming a design company. Don't do it on your own. Find a partner or partners.

As Quickhoney and e-boy illustrator Peter Stemmler says elsewhere in this book: 'Don't work alone.' Stemmler is a paradigm of industriousness and self-motivation, and his advice is sound: if you want to set up a successful design company, do it with a like-minded partner or partners. After all, it is much easier to share problems than shoulder them alone, and anything that increases the range of skills a studio can offer is valuable.

Once you've decided that having a business partner – or partners – is a good idea, all you have to do is find the right person or persons. To start with, you need to find people that you can get on with. You needn't be best friends (separate lives away from the studio is recommended), but you must choose people that you can work with at a sometimes alarming level of intimacy. You and your partners will be required, from time to time, to open yourselves up to intense personal scrutiny by each other. This doesn't tend to happen when times are good; when there are plenty of funds to go round everyone can afford to be generous. But when times are hard (as they frequently are) magnanimity is less easy. When money is scarce, business partners start to question each other's worth and to detect real or imagined signs of inequality and unfairness. So, you need to choose carefully: going into business with the wrong people can be expensive and emotionally destructive.

It will help if you share an ideological viewpoint with your partners. There needs to be some common ground, both creatively (the sort of work the studio is going to do and an overall policy relating to creative direction), and in the way you intend to conduct your business (business ethics and the way you treat staff, suppliers and the people you come into contact with). Now, I'm not advocating clone-like rigidity: you will never find partners who share your every view – and in truth, a degree of healthy disagreement is desirable. But you need to share broad principles because if you don't conflict will inevitably arise.

Of course, even when you've found your perfect partner, the hard work is only just beginning. Partnerships have to be tended, nurtured and repaired when damaged. In the early days, when you are high on the buzz of running your own studio, relationships with partners don't need much tending – you are too busy to worry about them. But remember: people change, and those ideals that you all signed up to at the beginning aren't necessarily the same ones you'll rally round in five to ten years' time. So, be flexible and be ready for change in yourself and in others.

61   *'I want to run my own studio. I like doing tax calculations and eighteen-hour days'*

Setting up a studio

Partnerships also need to be protected by written agreements: emotional chemistry isn't enough. A director's agreement, drawn up by a lawyer, is an important safeguard and a legal requirement in most countries. It may go against the spirit of communal endeavor in which your business was forged, but a legally binding exit strategy is mandatory. During the first thirteen years of Intro, I never once contemplated leaving; the company was my life. (My wife often said that she wished she was one of my clients: 'Then I'd see more of you.') But at some indefinable point I changed, and realized I wanted to leave and do other things. As it happened, since my departure was entirely amicable, it was managed without dispute. But had there been any disagreements about the terms of my leaving, then at least the directors had a document that defined the terms of our business partnership. I mention this solely to make the point that it is easy to imagine that as a co-owner you will remain committed to a company forever. But this is not necessarily the case.

Partnerships don't have to be equal. It is possible to have unequal shareholdings, distributed among two or more partners. This is a highly charged area with great potential for unhappiness and dissatisfaction. You will need to take careful advice on this aspect of your relationship. It is difficult to change the share structure of companies once they are in place. Tread cautiously and listen carefully to the advice you are given. Challenge any advice that doesn't feel correct or fair, but whatever you do, don't start off with the wrong partnership structure.

I've probably made the business of finding and choosing business partners sound more complicated – and risky – than it really is. In practice, most people manage it comfortably. In many cases, designers choose partners that they have already worked with. This makes sense, since they have already proved to each other that they can function as a team. It is what I did before starting Intro; I had worked for a medium-sized design company, and after a few years I came to the realization that I could do things better than the people who employed me and that my next step would be to run my own studio. But I wasn't so cocky that I thought I could do it without help. I knew my weaknesses.

Working in the same company, at that time, was a bright and energetic woman named Katy Richardson. We didn't have a great deal to do with each other, but we occasionally discussed our then employer's shortcomings. We discovered that we shared a creative and business vision of how a company should be run, and – most importantly – how its employees should be treated. One day Katy said: 'Would you like to set up a company together?' I thought about it for half a second and said yes. I recognized in her the skills that I lacked. She was an unusual combination of talents. When I joined the company she was the firm's bookkeeper. After a couple of years she'd taught herself film production and was promoted to head of production for the company's film and animation team. But most importantly, Katy had two skills that were to prove invaluable: she was financially astute and she knew about film production. I was financially retarded,[1] but I knew about design. Bingo – the perfect combination with which to set up a graphic design and moving-image company.

In his lecture, 'Tomato – A New Model for Creative Enterprise,' delivered to the Royal Society of Arts, Tomato Managing Director Steve Baker said the following: 'I have often been motivated by seeing frustrated potential and have for a long time thought that most creative people have extreme difficulty in exploiting their own talents. Many of them have tremendous problems handling money and sometimes get embarrassed just by having to talk about it. They usually undersell themselves or occasionally go to the opposite extreme, pricing themselves out of the market, and become impossible to trade with.' From *On Design and Innovation,* 1999.

This 'division of responsibilities' was the key to our success as a partnership. As one of our clients put it to me: 'She's money, you're art.' As we grew and brought new people into the company, this division of duties became more sophisticated. Over time, we employed a bookkeeper, an IT person and project managers (overseen by Katy), and also designers and someone to do new business (overseen by me).

There is a widespread misapprehension that designers make poor business-people. Not so. In fact designers are often good at business, and many design businesses are paradigms of efficiency and progressive practice. But if the thought of cash flow, sales projections, dealing with the bank and dealing with tax officials fills you with fear and loathing then you will need help. Someone needs to take responsibility for day-to-day financial affairs, and with that comes a serious responsibility. This person must be trustworthy, open and accountable. When you start to make money you can employ a good external accountant and a good in-house bookkeeper to help, but until then, you or one of your partners will have to do it. Competence in financial affairs is as important to a design company as good design skills, as Rudy VanderLans notes elsewhere in this book. VanderLans pays a warm tribute to his wife Zuzana Licko's 'terrific knack for detail and accounting, which is an absolute must. Bean counting is a major key to the success of any business.'

To ensure efficiency, partners should each take responsibility for different areas. For example, if there are three of you, you might choose to allocate your responsibilities as follows (other formulations are, of course, possible):

Partner 1   Creative direction, clients, new business and press relations
Partner 2   Financial affairs, studio manager, job costing and staff relations
Partner 3   Design, project management, IT and environmental policy

This allocation of responsibilities allows companies to grow and function without the partners treading on each other's toes. It doesn't mean that you don't communicate or that you stop sharing decision-making. Nor does it mean there is no overlap. On the contrary, when a studio is fighting to get itself off the ground everyone must be prepared to do whatever is most pressing. But life will be easier if each partner takes ultimate responsibility for a particular area.

If, for example, a studio computer dies and needs to be replaced, Partner 3 should deal with it. He or she needs to decide the type of new machine required, and liaises with Partner 2 about the cost. Partner 1 is then informed of their decision, and if all three are in agreement, Partner 3 orders the new machine and takes responsibility for its integration into the studio. And since Partner 3 is also responsible for the company's 'environmental policy', Partner 3 must oversee the responsible – and legal – disposal of the old machine. Meanwhile, Partner 1 had better be getting some work through the door, or Partners 2 and 3 will have something to complain about.

When each partner knows his or her responsibilities it is easy to get things done efficiently and this reduces the likelihood of accusations of inactivity being leveled at each other. As you grow, you might want to look at more sophisticated management and organizational techniques, but in the early days of a studio's existence you will need simple procedures that allow you to get work in and back out as chargeable product with maximum efficiency. And in a shape that you can be proud of.

63   *'I want to run my own studio. I like doing tax calculations and eighteen-hour days'*

Setting up a studio

Having eulogized the benefits of partnerships, it must be acknowledged that many good design companies are run by individuals. If you are the sort of super-confident designer who doesn't need a partner, good luck to you. My bet is, however, that you will get lonely sometimes: all that decision-making and no-one to share it with. And there are other models for the design group. You need to study them all and decide which best fits your circumstances. They all have legal implications so you must decide carefully. Steve Baker of Tomato describes the collectivist nature of the celebrated London company: 'Tomato acts very much like an agency, negotiating fees, invoicing and chasing for payment, and retaining a percentage before paying through to the individuals concerned. Much of the way that Tomato works is based on trust. There is no need for complicated written agreements between ourselves, and our shareholders agreement, which we have to have by law, includes such phrases as "enlightened self-interest" and "love." This is clearly an unconventional way of doing business and I am often faced with the blank stares of people who just don't get it.'

Published in
On Design
and Innovation, 1999.

Creating a business plan

To fund the setting up of a studio you might need to raise money. You should avoid borrowing a large amount unless you are extremely confident about your ability to generate cash to repay the loan. It is much better to start small, and if possible use savings to fund initial purchases. One of the great joys of graphic design is that you don't need vast amounts of money to get started. You need a computer, some software, a color printer, a scanner and a place to work. You will also need a good broadband internet connection, some smart stationery and a supply of stimulants (caffeine or other) to keep you awake at night as you do the obligatory all-nighters. Even this modest outlay shouldn't be underestimated. If there are two or three of you, you need to multiply the costs proportionately. As designers, we are lucky; the price of entry into professional life is not prohibitive. But neither is it free. If you need to raise money from a bank you will need a business plan. Even if you don't need funding, prepare a business plan anyway. Nothing sobers you up quicker than a poke in the eye from a sharp business plan. But it is only by doing an accurate calculation – projected income against projected expenditure with ample contingencies for the unforeseen – that you will know what you have to do to survive. It will be daunting, and you must be ruthlessly honest with yourself. Assume the worst. Assume that your income will be abysmal and your expenditure substantial. It will make you wince with pain, but it will be the brutal reality check you need before embarking on life as the owner of a design company. You can get help with business plans from a number of commercial and government agencies. The latter provide instructions on how to compile a business plan – and they are free. See the appendix at the end of the book for some useful websites.

3   The independent business turnaround specialist John Dewhirst, a former financial director of a leading design company, wrote in *Design Week* (24 July, 2003): 'There are three fundamental lessons to be learned about business failure. The first is that failure is due to a lack of cash rather than a lack of reported profit (cash is a matter of fact while profit is a matter of opinion). The second is that once a business is on a trend of under-performance, there is often a rapid acceleration into crises and ultimate demise. The third is that business failure is rarely due to a sudden or unforeseen catastrophe – time and again the same shortcomings lead to decline: defects in management, inadequate financial systems and controls, over-commitments and strategic or structural deficiencies.'

A good accountant can do a business plan for you, but try to do it yourself and get an accountant to check it. Doing it yourself will make it more relevant, and more real to you. Be tough on yourself, assume bad things will happen.[3] Assume you will have more expenses than income; assume you will have fewer clients than you hoped for; assume that you will be paid more slowly than you'd like; assume that you will have at least one bad debt in your first year. Not deceiving yourself is the secret of business planning. If you are realistic and pragmatic in the running of your business, you can afford to be cavalier in your creative life.

Professional advisers and services

You will need a bank, there's no ducking this one. You will almost certainly already have a bank, and there are advantages (and disadvantages) in sticking with an institution that already knows you. Of course, a business account is different from a personal one, and to open a business account you need to speak to a bank manager. Ask friends and fellow designers to recommend someone; arrange to meet a few managers before deciding which bank suits you. Bank managers are no longer the ogre-like figures they once were. They have become part of the service sector and they want your business. The days of feeling small and insignificant in the face of your bank manager are over. Most banks have helpful start-up packs for new businesses, and a good manager will guide you through the first steps of launching a business – if he or she doesn't, ditch them and find one who will.

For the fledgling design company, having a good accountant is like having a good analyst. It is also a legal requirement that an incorporated company submits professionally accredited accounts, so there's no doing without an accountant. The main benefit, though, is having someone to talk to and someone who will listen to you about business concerns. A good accountant should save you more money than his or her services cost, so it's worth getting a good one, even if good ones are more expensive than mediocre ones. I recommend that you choose one on the basis of personal recommendation and personal chemistry. As always, ask around and get some names from friends. You need someone who will be friendly but ruthlessly dispassionate. You need someone who will always tell you the truth, even when it hurts. You also need someone who will not be patronising. An accountant who treats you like an idiot is no use. Ditch them.

65   *'I want to run my own studio. I like doing tax calculations and eighteen-hour days'*

Setting up a studio

As with your bank manager, it is also a good idea to have an accountant who has other designers as clients. Although this is by no means obligatory, it is worth, in the early days of your career, choosing one who knows about design. And don't be intimidated by him or her. Ask how much they charge, and when they charge. Ask if you can speak to one or two of their existing clients for a reference (if they say no, be suspicious), and get them to say exactly what they will do for you.

You will also need a lawyer. You find lawyers in exactly the same way you find an accountant. With any luck you will speak to your lawyer only rarely. Speaking to lawyers is expensive, and we tend to do it only when we are in trouble.

Starting up

You've found a partner – or partners – and you've negotiated a partnership agreement. You've made a business plan. You've found a bank, and you've got an accountant. Having done all this, you'd have thought you could now start earning a living and doing what you do best – designing. Not yet, first you have some practical matters to take care of. Your accountant will tell you what these are, and how and when to do them; but it's worth looking at a list of the most important things you need to do to launch a company.

1   Register your business with the relevant authorities
2   Register your company name and secure a URL
3   Set up relevant payroll and tax status
4   Issue employment contracts to staff
5   Create client contracts to protect intellectual property

I asked an accountant with experience in advising design studios to summarize the essentials of good financial management for a graphic design practice. Amanda Merron is a partner in accounting firm Willott Kingston Smith: she has numerous design and media-related clients and regularly offers guidance in the pages of *Design Week*. I've always found her advice to be clear, comprehensible and helpful. All accountants should be this good. She suggests having a clear focus on what the business offers and how it can be effectively delivered. This knowledge will go a long way towards ensuring success in a design business. When it comes to managing your finances, she points out that there are three key areas:

1   Planning

Business planning and budgeting is often seen as a difficult, even scary, process which only accountants can tackle. This is far from the case. It is simply saying what you think is likely to happen in terms of cost and income, and writing it down. This is not an exact process – in fact the most accurate thing you can say is that it will be wrong. It makes sense to consider which of the assumptions made is most likely to change and assess the impact of that.

Having written a sensible plan, actual business performance should be measured against what you thought was going to happen. Trying to measure performance in isolation is practically impossible. Is an income of $100,000 for the year good? Not if you expected $200,000, but if you had only planned for $75,000 you might be pleased. What should be reported? Key elements are as follows:

	Plan $	Actual $	Difference $
Fee income	100,000	80,000	(20,000)
Cost	(50,000)	(50,000)	–
Profit	50,000	30,000	(20,000)
Bank balance	40,000	20,000	(20,000)

As well as looking back to see what happened it is vital to look forward to consider what new work might be coming in, how much cash is likely to be needed and so on, on a regular basis.

3 Reacting

Any significant deviation from plan should be investigated and something done about it. For example, if income is lower than anticipated, can you raise your fees or cut costs somewhere.

Finding an office

You will need an office. If you've got the space, you might start off by working from home. Even if you haven't got the space, consider working from home anyway; set up in your bedroom, your garage, your garden shed or your kitchen until you've got some income flowing in the direction of your bank account. Only then should you consider acquiring an office, or staff, or that Gaggia coffee machine. Most clients won't mind you working from home; they can be surprisingly generous and supportive towards start-ups, and often like to be seen to be helping young design teams get started – especially if they think you are going to be cheaper than established companies. Anyway, as long as you are prepared to visit them every time they want a meeting, they needn't know where you're based. In the new wi-fi world, we can be anywhere we want to be.

But at some point, you will want to find a space that enables you to set up a proper studio. A good way to start is by talking to other designers, especially designers who already rent space. They will sometimes know of opportunities that are available via their existing landlords. Also, larger studios sometimes sublet space. Again, this will do while you are getting your studio established, but as you grow a cuckoo-like existence within another studio will feel unsatisfactory, and you will want to move on. There's a scene in Dave Eggers' book *A Heartbreaking Work of Staggering Genius,* which many designers will find vividly familiar. Eggers describes the hassles of renting studio space in which to produce a magazine. In doing so, he offers another sort of arrangement (a slightly eccentric one, it has to be admitted) for a graphic design start-up: 'We move our offices from our condemned warehouse to the fifth floor of a glassy office box in the middle of the city. The [San Francisco] *Chronicle* promotions department, wanting us close so Moodie and I can provide lightning-

67   *'I want to run my own studio. I like doing tax calculations and eighteen-hour days'*

Setting up a studio

quick service, have let us move in with them … giving us about 800 square feet, with floor-to-ceiling windows, for $1,000 a month – which Moodie and I easily pay by overcharging them for our design work.' Pro bono arrangements are a good idea, but only to get you started and then after that only in carefully controlled circumstances: tolerance is soon exhausted, and disgruntlement can quickly set in. And be wary of following Eggers' fictional example and overcharging: this tactic has a way of coming back to bite you.

How do you know how much space to rent? Ask designer friends who run their own studios. Go and visit small studios and get a feel for space in relation to number of bodies. Once you've established a good people-to-space ratio, make do with less space than you'd like: you won't mind being cramped for the first few months. Take a short lease so that you can walk away if everything goes wrong, or so that you can trade up if you start to do well.

Making friends – rather than enemies – with the people you encounter in professional life is a good policy. At Intro, we started life in a tiny office at the top of a large building. Hardly smart, the rooms were adequate for our first eighteen months. At the end of our tenancy we were doing well; we had work, a steady income and good prospects (it was a boom time in the UK for design). As a consequence of this early success we felt confident enough to rent a large building on five floors in central London. The rent was hefty, but if we carried on doing as well as we had been we could cover it comfortably. And for a year or so, we did. We enjoyed having a large building that allowed everyone plenty of space, and gave us, as a company, a bit of swagger. Big mistake. We hit the early-nineties economic downturn with a Titanic-like thump. Our income shrunk, and we found ourselves with a rent that we could barely cope with.

But we had a trump card. The young real estate agent who had found the building for us had become a friend. We were one of his first transactions; he was ambitious and dynamic and had taken a shine to us. We approached him for help. He went to the building's owners and negotiated a reduced rent on our behalf. He did this because we'd treated him with respect during the transaction, and because he could see that we were a serious and ambitious group of people who'd doubtless make another move soon, and when we did we'd award him the task of finding a new office for us. Don't rely on this happening if you get into trouble; acts of disinterested kindness are rare in business, and even rarer in the world of real estate. We had a lucky break, and without it we might not have survived. But we got lucky because we'd made a friend of our property adviser. Friends are better than enemies is the only lesson here.

Choosing a name

You've made your move. You've set up on your own. You've bought enough computer kit (your accountant advised you on the best method to pay for it) to compete with NASA, and you've found an office (you're next door to a twenty-four-hour pizza parlor, and there was a guy asleep on your doorstep this morning clutching a bottle of something that smelled like lighter fuel mixed with urine, but it's your office and you love it). Now you must choose a name. Fashions in design group names change constantly. I can't offer much advice here other than to remind you that you will have to live with your chosen name for a long time. In years to come you might change the nature of your business so you don't want to be saddled with a name that is inappropriate. It's worth remembering that names pass into a sort of barely visible neutrality after a while. Like a new pair of shoes, a new name feels stiff and conspicuous to start with, but just as you soon 'grow into' new shoes and they become part of your skin, so too with names. Unless, of course, you choose something really stupid.

Identity

Once you've got your name, you must start work on a studio identity. Dragging a grand piano up Everest with your teeth will be easier, but you've got to do it. Try and get it right, because it can't easily be changed once you've decided. Few things will vex you quite as much as creating your studio's identity – it exposes a weakness in the mentality of most designers. We are generally bad at designing for ourselves. Designers spend their working lives telling their clients how to cultivate an appropriate image, yet seem paralyzed when they have to do it for themselves. It doubtless has something to do with the deep-seated notion that to be a designer you need a brief. And although there's a rise in the number of designers who initiate their own projects, there is nonetheless a deep biological impulse in most designers that says 'I can't work without a brief.'

But short of inviting a friend – or another design company – to design your own identity, you have to get on with it, and you have to do it well. The best way to do this is to treat it like a job from a client. Agree among yourselves who is going to do it, then write a proper brief with objectives, schedules and budgets, and make it into a real live job. When it's done, assess the results with detachment and objectivity. In fact, do everything that you would do with an external job, except send yourself a bill.

Studio systems

Designers are often resistant to excessive bureaucracy. Quite right too. If your day is spent filling in time sheets and other tiresome administrative tasks, you won't have much time – or appetite – for creative work. But it is another paradox in the life of a designer that we are at our most free when we are at our most organized.

There are a number of good books and guides to studio administration and studio management. I've listed some in the bibliography at the end of this book. But more importantly, there are people you can employ to organize your studio for you. These are wonderful individuals – visionary individuals – with the god-like skill of organization. But until you can afford one of these administration-deities (they can often be hired part-time), it is essential that you undertake the basic requirements of organization yourself.

Here's a list of what you need to do: it gives the basic organizational necessities for keeping track of your work, your costs and your income. As you grow, you will come to do this effortlessly. But to get started, and to keep on top of your studio's performance, here is what you need:

1   A system for booking work in
2   A system for allocating costs
3   A system for allocating project numbers to all jobs
4   A system for allocating project numbers to all in-house jobs
5   A system for ordering studio supplies (blank CDs, computers and tea/coffee)
6   A system for monitoring cash flow, which includes debt chasing
7   A system for paying salaries, suppliers and rent
8   A system for monitoring work flow
9   An IT network with software for administration and accounting support

How to be a graphic designer, without losing your soul

John Warwicker

John Warwicker graduated from Camberwell School of Arts in London. During the 1980s he was briefly a member of the band Freuer (who later became Underworld); was part of the design group da Gama; and was art director of A&M Records. After a stint as head of the 'information design company' Vivid, Warwicker formed the creative collective Tomato with Steve Baker, Dirk Van Dooren, Simon Taylor, Graham Wood, Jason Kedgley, Michael Horsham and Underworld members Richard Smith and Karl Hyde. Tomato works across film, branding, music, television, cinema, commercials, advertising, books, architecture and interactive media. They have exhibited internationally, and lecture and hold workshops widely. Clients include Sony, Nike, Levis, Coca-Cola and the Victoria & Albert Museum. In 2005, Warwicker will publish *The Floating World: Ukiyo-e*, the first monograph on his work. In it he documents his experiences in an authentic voice, mining the themes, ideas, histories and memories that have informed and influenced him over the past ten years.

www.tomato.co.uk

Designed
by Tomato

AS What prompted you to become a graphic designer? JW I don't know whether I've ever thought of myself as a 'graphic designer'. I do remember as a child being fascinated by my grandfather's mathematical notebooks and the strange letterforms in it. I'm sure that's where my love of typography started. And I do remember at the age of nine or ten designing my own newspaper in the weekly art classes in junior school. And like every teenager, music played a really important part in my cultural definition. Record sleeves were like flags of allegiance and in the early seventies they symbolized what 'graphic design' was to most of us growing up at that time. At art school I had the 'choice' between fine art and graphic design. My parents supported me throughout my education, which was quite hard for them. I was worried that I couldn't earn enough money from 'fine art', at least in the initial stages, and I didn't want to be a further burden on them. I thought that I would probably earn enough to pay my way if I worked as a 'graphic designer'. For me 'graphic design' was a label someone else put on the work.

Looking back, how do you view your design education? Were there things that you didn't appreciate at the time, but which in retrospect have proved beneficial? Not really. My education at Camberwell School of Arts was comprehensive. I took the attitude, as did many of my peers, that art school was an opportunity to be fully embraced. We were very self-motivated and hungry for knowledge.

What were your ambitions at the start of your professional life? The same as they are now – to do something that I'm not expecting and that teaches me something about the world and my place in it.

You were involved in music industry design early on in your career. Was this a good grounding for what came later? No. I'm afraid it confirmed my suspicions of any creative group that calls itself an 'industry'.

You are famous for being a designer who disregards the conventional boundaries of design. You make books, films, installations and interactive work. You write prose and you give talks and lectures. Can you talk about this? What boundaries? It's my life and I do what I'm interested in or intrigued by. If anyone else is interested, that's good – maybe there will be a conversation.

Tomato members are celebrated for mixing personal projects with commercial work. What does this give the individual? Their individuality!

What is the most important lesson you have learned as a graphic designer? That there's no such thing as 'graphic design'. Only lots of books on it and an assumption that it exists. And that the world likes to 'commodify'.

What advice would you give to a designer starting out today? Find your own voice. And find out what motivates others.

How to be a graphic designer, without losing your soul

I read an interview in which you said: 'Tell your clients when they are wrong. Because sometimes they are.' Is this good advice for a young designer? Shouldn't they be doing what they are told? No. They should think about what is being proposed and see if they agree with it. And if they don't agree, they should say so in a quiet and reasonable way. Ask 'Why?' of both yourself and the client. If you don't, you won't learn and neither will the client. What's important is to build a portfolio that does not have to be qualified. It should speak for itself. I know this through bitter experience. In the 1980s I won awards and the 'industry' liked my work. I gave a talk at St. Martins and this very large guy with a goatee and woolly hat approached me afterwards. He said that he really enjoyed what I said, but thought my work was 'crap.' He was right. And that's how I met Graham (Wood) who I later formed Tomato with. I made a mental note to throw away ten years of work, but it took me several years to completely let go. You have to pull yourself up every day and erase old habits. I've never been satisfied with any of the 'commercial' work that I've ever done.

What is good about the young designers you see, and what, if anything, is lacking? The good ones have energy. The not-so-good ones lack discipline, knowledge, self-criticism and are too reliant on technology. But I think this is true for every designer, no matter what age.

OK, you can't really
design a car in
a few hours, but you
get what I'm saying
here: design
can't be automated.

The secret of success in running a design company is treating the people the company employs like gods. This reads like the sort of vacuous fluff you find in cheap business-management books or corporate employee manuals, but it's true. Despite the near total computerization of the design process, design is still the product of individual minds. It's one of the reasons why design is such an attractive career proposition today. In design, unlike so many other areas of contemporary life, the individual is still at the center of everything. You can build a car in a fraction of the time it takes to make a decent piece of graphic design: this is because the making of cars, unlike the making of graphic design, is fully automated. Despite the ubiquity of the Apple computer, design is still something you do with hand, eye and brain. It's why designers become unhappy when their work is mutilated by clients, and why they become elated when their work is successful and lauded.

If you want to run a design studio, you will need to employ staff. This isn't to say you have to become a vast empire with an endless number of employees, far from it. It is a recurring theme in interviews with good designers that they rarely express a desire to run a large studio; 'small is beautiful' seems to be the ethos of the independent-minded designer. And if you want to be an independent-minded designer (and not lose your soul in the process) then you almost certainly will want to stay small, employing only a handful of designers.

Growth is the great conundrum of modern graphic design. Designers say to themselves: if I become big, I will lose my independence and I will be forced to take on work I don't want to do simply to cover my overheads. But as the great Tibor Kalman said: 'The toughest thing when running a studio is not to grow'. Kalman should have added 'if you are any good' to that sentence – and 'good' is the key word here. If you are any good, you will attract more work than you can easily cope with, and if you are any good, growth – and by growth I mean taking on more people – is unavoidable. I'm talking here about having the confidence to add to a small team to enable you to do better work and cope with the escalating demands of surviving in a harsh business environment. As all the business books point out, companies only have two gears, forward and reverse, and standing still is the same as going backwards. So, even if your goal is to stay small and focused, you cannot allow your company to stand still. You have to go forward, and to do this you need to frequently enrich your creative gene-pool by employing people who add skills and brainpower to your studio.

Running a studio means all-night working and marathon sessions spent in front of the computer screen – while all the time desperately trying to maintain standards of quality and delivery. Designers tend not to complain about this. If you were to try and take those long hours away from them, they would resist. It's part of the joy of doing something that they love. But eventually it catches up with you – you may begin to make mistakes and clients will spot the drop in quality. Taking on staff to help you cope with increased demand needn't be a death sentence – you just have to know how to do it, and how to do it well.

Employing creative staff

In a previous chapter I looked at how tough it is for the new designer to find a job, but spare a moment for the poor employer: it is just as tough finding good employees. Getting the right people – partners, design staff, non-design staff – is the one thing a start-up design studio can't afford to get wrong. It's possible to screw up in every other area and still prosper, but in recruitment you can't afford to make mistakes. In this chapter I'll look at ways to find, assess and secure talent. And then I'll discuss how to treat the people we work with, because it is not enough to find and hire talented people, we have to nurture them.

When you set up in business, you are offered lots of advice. When I co-founded Intro, I discounted most of the advice I was given by well-meaning acquaintances and business people, because I wanted to trust my common sense and intuition. I wanted to find new and fresh ways of doing things, and I figured that if I listened to everything I was told I'd be force-fed a lot of old-fashioned formulaic thinking. I also felt that 'design was different', and I was loath to take guidance from anyone who didn't know about design, and the quirks and slightly wonky logic of the design world. And of course, I was more arrogant than I am now, and wrongly imagined I didn't need the help of outsiders.

However, one piece of advice that I was offered struck me as perversely good. In fact, so good that much later I found it to be the single most helpful piece of advice anyone gave me concerning the running of a design studio. It came from an unlikely source, too – an acquaintance who had made numerous attempts to become a successful businessman, all of which had ended in failure, and who knew nothing about design or designers. He told me: 'Always employ people who are *better than you.*'

At a critical stage in the development of Intro, we experimented with a management consultant: he advised a course of restructuring that didn't seem to fit into our flatter, more democratic structure. I asked him why he'd recommended this approach. He looked miffed, and replied: 'Well, because it's what everyone else does.' Bad answer. Needless to say, we didn't take his advice, and after he showed us an 'instructional' video which used McDonald's corporate practices as its basis, we decided not to retain his services.

Did the earth move for you when you read this? It didn't for me when I first heard it, although it was eventually to become my first rule of creative recruitment. I suspect for designers, perhaps recruiting for the first time in their careers, it is tough advice to swallow. Designers are a vulnerable breed; easily discouraged, easily damaged and quick to feel threatened. Not many designers willingly agree to be upstaged by new talent in their own backyard. Personally, I wrestled with this notion for a long time before finding the courage to put it into practice. But as soon as I did, I saw it for the great truism it is. And when I saw the benefits of employing designers more talented than myself, I was able to concentrate on the things I did best (creative direction and working with clients).

Now, I'm aware that formulations like 'better than' are largely redundant in design. What does it mean if you say that someone is a 'better designer' than someone else? Not much; to have any meaning it would have to be accompanied by caveats and elaborate qualifiers. But what my well-intentioned advice-giver meant was that employing people who have skills and abilities that you lack is the only way to ensure a studio's growth and development. It allows you to offer more to clients, and it allows you to delegate some of the tasks you've been struggling to perform, enabling you to concentrate on the things that you do best.

This brings us to the second rule of creative recruitment. This harsh-sounding rule states that any employee who is any good will leave. Now, on the surface, this is not good news: who wants to employ people, no matter how talented, if they are going to up and leave? Yet the notion of departing talent has a hidden benefit, and the hidden benefit is that because the departure of talent is an inevitability, you are therefore obliged to operate a perpetual search for fresh talent. Employers and studio heads tend to only interview prospective employees when they need to. This is short-sighted. See people all the time: see every designer worth seeing and scout constantly for good people. If you do this, you'll greatly reduce your exposure when the inevitable happens and key members of staff leave.

The unwanted departure of key people is often traumatic, but it needn't be permanently damaging. Always remember that you are in one of the richest talent pools in the modern world. In our hyper-educated society, any number of people want to work in the creative industries. The art colleges are producing record numbers of graduates and this means that there is unlikely to be a shortage of talent – in fact, there's a glut. Think big, don't be frightened. If you lose a key member of the team there is always someone else to replace them.

Now, I'm not advocating complacency here. There are many, many things you can do to reduce the risk of losing people, and it is sensible to do these things. You can pay better salaries than other studios. You can offer better benefits and more congenial working conditions. You can offer key staff members equity in your company. In the early days of your studio, you will have no time for these matters and you will barely be able to consider them. These fiscal benefits need to be planned carefully, and should be part of an overall financial plan for your company. You will need the help of your accountant here, and you will need to tread carefully and thoughtfully. Employing staff is a bit like having children. Suddenly, you have to become less selfish.

But your commitment to staff – especially design staff – doesn't end with fiscal matters. The most important thing you can offer a designer is good work. This will override most feelings of restlessness, even if it sometimes means that, as a studio, you have to take on work that is not profitable, but which offers designers a chance to create the sort of work they want to do.

There are other things you can do to demonstrate your commitment to staff. For instance: it is sometimes necessary to back an individual designer at the expense of a client. If a client is being unreasonable, and if the designer has done everything within his or her powers to ensure a satisfactory outcome, then you must back the designer and sack the client. I've done this on a number of occasions and it has paid off. Designers recognize the sacrifice that has been made and repay the gesture with renewed energy and commitment. [3] Naturally, you need to be careful here, because if you start sacking clients every time they upset a member of your design team, you will have no business left. But a bad client can cause as much damage as a good one can bring benefits. Knowing when to sack a client is a matter of careful judgment.

3   I once sacked a client whose behavior towards one of our designers was unreasonable. When I told the designer what I'd done, she begged me to change my mind and said that she didn't mind having her life made miserable, after all. From then on I always checked with the designer before sacking a client.

Is there anything less drastic you can do to show commitment to your designers? At Intro, we allowed designers to have personal credits on the work they produced, and made sure they were name-checked when the company's work was featured in magazines. Encouraging designers to sign their work (a credit would read: Designed by John Smith, Intro) flies in the face of conventional wisdom, which states that you keep your designers hidden. You should only ever promote the firm's brand name, and you should never allow employees to develop a profile – they'll only be poached or become big-headed. But far from encouraging poaching or big-headedness, personal credits on work and mentions in the design press do exactly the opposite. They create loyalty and openness. Through the implementation of this simple device, designers are able to achieve peer recognition and derive a sense of personal authorship, as well as having something tangible to show their mothers and friends.

This policy of encouraging personal credits has to be balanced by the fact that a great many design projects are jointly authored; many individuals – designers and non-designers – may contribute to a project's success (in these instances, the signature on work read Design by Intro). As a precaution, I retained the right to change a credit if I felt it was unmerited. In practice, I never had to do this.

This brings me to the third rule of creative recruitment. It was given to me by a successful businessman friend. Like the advice from my less successful acquaintance, it seemed to sneer at common sense. This is what he told me: 'People who want to have their own businesses make the best employees. Never be frightened to employ people who ultimately want to start their own studios. Think about it,' he said, 'it's what you did.'

Surely people who want to start their own businesses will leave you in the lurch as soon as it suits them? Well, maybe. But the reason this is good advice is that we need to employ able and ambitious people (people who are better than us). And, anyway, at Intro we operated – from day one – a policy of constantly interviewing and scouting for new talent, so replacement was made easier.

It is a good idea to instigate a regular program of portfolio viewing. Try and see two or three people each month. You will need to be frank with your interviewees and state that you have agreed to see them because you are 'planning ahead;' and you need to tell your existing staff, who may feel threatened by the regularity with which you view the work of other designers, that it is your policy to constantly view portfolios. It is one of the ways you future-proof your studio.

In the early days of Intro (when there were only four or five of us) I did many different jobs: from changing light bulbs to unblocking toilets. I stayed up all night designing record covers for stroppy record labels who sent copy in at 9 pm and wanted finished artwork twelve hours later; I was even threatened with violence by an enraged window cleaner (I mention this only to make the point that when you start up a design company you have to do anything and everything – even deal with unstable window cleaners). Most design studios start like this: you do everything yourself until you can afford some help.

My adviser gave me another dollop of wisdom. He told me to 'only employ people who are married with children and mortgages – they are more reliable. Less likely to upset the apple cart.' I like people who upset apple carts, so I ignored this advice.

But how do you know when to employ more staff? This is a matter of careful judgment. You don't want to employ people if you don't have any work for them. Similarly, you don't want to expire from overwork yourself, or lose opportunities to take on new and interesting work, because you are understaffed. Furthermore, if you try and do everything yourself (which is the right thing to do when starting out), you will not only exhaust yourself, but you will start to produce sub-standard work, and you will inevitably lose clients. Employing new people at key moments (even if it is only one person a year) will bring about growth and development; failure to do so will mean, at best, that you don't have enough help to run your studio, and at worse that you run the risk of staying permanently in neutral gear.

Early on at Intro, our policy was only to recruit when we had a steady flow of guaranteed work. This was fine as a start-up policy, but since, as I've already noted, new designers can take time to get up to speed, it was only partially successful as a strategy. After a while, when we grew in confidence and our financial situation improved, we'd take on staff *ahead of anticipated need*. This allowed new people to get up to speed, and it meant that we had an added incentive to get new projects in through the door.

To bring in new staff without careful financial planning, and without the confidence that you will generate enough work for them, is dangerous. My advice is to be cautious, but be brave too. Whatever you do, don't do nothing.

Having employed dozens of designers, I've never once taken into account a candidate's academic qualification. I might take into account which design school an applicant attended, but I'm not swayed by the quality of degree. This is not to say that other employers don't take academic status into account, nor am I saying I don't value the effort that students put into obtaining a degree. I just know that too many good designers achieved poor grades at design school, and it is always worth looking beyond academic marks.

Spotting talent

When you interview a designer you are looking for three things; talent, suitability and potential. How do you spot these qualities? I'm tempted to say that when you see them, you know them, but that seems a bit too casual. Yet intuition – experience – plays a big part. Perhaps the best way to learn to spot an individual's qualities is to make some mistakes. I was once asked by a British design school to set a competition and in a fit of generosity (we were doing well) I said that I'd also offer the winner a job. When the results came through, there were two astonishing pieces of work with nothing to choose between either. I found myself with two winners. I interviewed the two students, and I ended up employing both of them.

One of the two proved to be an able and talented individual who stayed with us for a number of years; the other was a disaster and had to be asked to leave at the end of his first week. I had been seduced by the designer's work (his talent), and I'd forgotten to properly assess his character (suitability and potential). The point I'm making here is that you have to be careful when employing people, and you have to look for signs beyond the pages of their portfolios. You can take references from previous employers, though this is less easy in the case of recent graduates where you have to rely on intuition. And nothing sharpens up your judgment like an expensive mistake.

As we can see from the example given above, it is essential to introduce a probationary period (usually three months) in which to monitor the performance of an individual. Here we are getting into the tricky area of employment law, which you need to be vigilant about. Generally speaking, adhering to employment law means no more than doing the things we'd want to do anyway as responsible employers. They vary from nation to nation, but typically, and rightly, employment legislation strongly supports the rights of employees. Be certain your employment contracts are airtight and that you honor health and safety laws.

How do you spot talent and how do you make sure you find the person who's right for you? To find people who fit, you could try doing what Bruce Mau did – post a forty-question cultural trivia quiz on your website and invite candidates to demonstrate their suitability by answering as many of the questions as they can. Here are a few of Mau's questions: What is the difference between nigri and sashimi? Who designed the CNN logo? What artist founded the Chinati Foundation in Marfa, Texas? What text by Guy Debord was central to the events of May 1968?

But, in truth, you don't spot it, it spots you. Think about it. Good designers only approach good studios; anyone with any talent is only going to be attracted to a studio or a firm with a good reputation. If you have a good reputation, talent will find you.

Non-design staff

Employing non-creative staff (administrators, studio managers, receptionists, project managers, producers, etc.) is just like employing creative staff. You have to choose people who are sympathetic to the culture of your studio, which is much easier to do than it once was: now that design is seen as a more glamorous and desirable occupation, non-designers are happy to work in design studios.

You will only start to think about employing non-design staff once you've grown to a size where your workload is threatening to overwhelm you, and where it has become economically viable to employ people who are not, primarily, fee-generating. It was a surprise to discover that the more non-fee-generating people we employed at Intro, the more our fee-earners generated. At first, I was resistant to employing non-designers; I couldn't see the logic of employing non-fee-generating people. Surely it would reduce our profitability? In fact, thanks to my business partner's perceptiveness, the improved efficiency that came from employing talented and able support staff meant that more work was done (with no drop in quality) and more income generated.

Almost certainly a bookkeeper should be your first non-creative appointment. You might next think about some sort of project manager, studio manager or production person. Employing someone with project management skills can free designers from administrative, production and financial chores. The model we had at Intro was based on the producer/director model common in film and moving-image production. We didn't assign one designer to one project manager, but one project manager looked after two to three designers. Again, I was resistant to this formula at first. I'd always done my own production – liaised with printers, costed jobs, negotiated with clients – and I believed that it made designers stronger if they had this experience. I still believe that designers, in the early stages of their careers, benefit from having to do their own production – but it's doubtful whether many of them are much good at it, and the benefits of partnering designers with project managers are unquestionable.

Project managers – or a studio manager – should take control of all production matters relating to a job (helping with presentations, preparing costings, negotiating budgets, controlling paperwork, scheduling around other work, monitoring progress, dealing with printers and other external suppliers, invoicing and remembering to charge for extras – something designers notoriously forget to do). This is also a good way to deal with difficult clients. Designers play good cop, project managers play bad cop. Project managers can have those prickly conversations with clients about budgets, delayed schedules and payment wrangles, leaving designers free to talk about the project at hand.

Project managers used to be hard to find, but they are plentiful today. As the business of design grows and design firms proliferate, more studios employ the services of project managers and the pool of experienced talent has increased. The good ones often come from big design groups where they have been well trained, and where they have gained experience working on large-scale projects, and yet perhaps have been frustrated by the 'corporate' nature of life in a big design company.

Big design companies often employ account handlers. I've never been a fan of the notion of account managers. I'm sure there are good ones, and I know there are clients who will pay handsomely to have a dedicated account handler looking after them. But I've never been a convert to the concept. I saw the problems caused by account handlers when I dealt with advertising agencies, where they are powerful figures. I've worked on projects with creative teams in agencies, and watched as work is handed over to an account handler to be presented to the client. Since he or she has no personal investment in the work they show, if the client doesn't like the work, they have no way of defending it. They simply bring it back like a dog with a bone and deposit it at the feet of the creative team, and say 'rejected.' I began this book by advising designers 'to strive to see the client's point of view,' which is not the same as getting into bed with the client. But that is what account handlers do; they become split in their loyalties and the split is rarely even – it is biased in favor of the client.

The notion of offering escape to 'refugees' from corporate hell was one of my guiding principles at Intro. I made a point of always interviewing designers from corporate backgrounds – they were invariably highly competent and disciplined individuals, and often itching to move into a more expressive and less restrictive environment. A period in a good design studio producing work for corporate clients can provide invaluable experience for a young designer, furnishing him or her with valuable skills and disciplines.

Account handlers also have the effect of making designers feel dislocated from the design process. Client contact is essential if designers are going to do meaningful work. I've already noted how beneficial it can be for designers to be removed from the direct responsibility of negotiating with clients over money and scheduling by the introduction of a good project manager or production person, but when a designer loses direct contact with the client he or she simply becomes less effective and less committed.

Receptionists

In the modern workplace the notion of a 'receptionist' is anachronistic, slightly old-fashioned. The businessman Ricardo Semler who turned his Brazilian company Semco into a blueprint for egalitarian and progressive working practices, wrote in his book *Maverick!*: 'We don't have receptionists. We don't think they are necessary, despite all our visitors. We don't have secretaries either, or personal assistants. We don't believe in cluttering the payroll with ungratifying, dead-end jobs. Everyone at Semco, even top managers, fetches guests, stands over photocopiers, sends faxes, types letters, and dials the phones … It's all part of running a "natural business."'

In the age of e-mail, mobile phones and sophisticated telephone systems, I'd say that Semler was on to something. But there's another consideration. With the right person in charge of 'front-of-house,' a studio's ability to deal with its clients, its visitors and random inquiries, is greatly enhanced. Think how many times you've rung a store, or a garage, or a utility company, and received a surly greeting. How did your view of that company change after the encounter?

Answering the phone quickly and in a friendly manner is vital in any service business. Welcoming studio visitors and arranging basic hospitality is important (actually, creative staff can do this just as well, except they are usually still finishing off the presentation that the client has come to see). But it's not just in the matter of answering the phone and looking after visitors that receptionists are important; it is also essential to have someone to act as a friendly gatekeeper to deal with pushy photocopier salesmen and shy job-seeking students. I believe strongly in the old-fashioned benefits of a good receptionist. I've worked with many over the years and the good ones always added something quantifiable to the way a studio looked after its clients and staff.

At what stage do you decide you need a receptionist? There is no hard and fast rule, but look at it this way: like most other roles, you can do it yourself or share the task among the others, but an unanswered phone or a badly answered phone is as effective as a recorded message saying, *'We don't want your business.'* So you need to think about acquiring a receptionist when you are generating enough calls to make it essential that you turn them into live jobs.

Adding staff alters the dynamics of a company. It might enable you to do more work, but it adds to your overhead and makes it imperative to increase turnover. This might mean losing some freedom: the freedom to turn away uncongenial work, for instance. All these factors need to be considered when deciding on adding staff. Just remember, not adding talent will result in stagnation at some point in the future, and new talent enriches the studio's gene pool.

Philosophy

As well as good people – and good work – studios need to have a philosophy; they need to have something they can believe in. And they need to have an ethical base on which to operate. In practice, this usually means that designers have a 'creative philosophy' backed up by 'business ethics' – although, when it comes to being a working graphic designer, the two are intertwined.

The Intro philosophy was to always do great work regardless of the budget. We told ourselves that there was no such thing as a bad job. Every job, we believed, had the potential to be an opportunity to add a great piece of work to our portfolio, and we believed that great work always gets noticed, and work that gets noticed leads to better assignments. It meant that we did low-budget work with the same enthusiasm and commitment that we applied to big-budget work because we knew that the small-budget work (it usually offered greater freedom, anyway) was our passport to bigger and better work.

We also allowed our designers to pursue their own creative visions – we didn't impose a studio straitjacket on them. In other words, there was no house style. Designers were free to be themselves creatively, with only one proviso: there had to be clients who wanted what they did. This philosophy made promoting Intro difficult. Drumming up new work with so many stylistic and conceptual voices on offer wasn't always easy. I often looked at studios and individuals with a consistent style and envied them. Surely their lives were much easier than ours, I thought. With us, clients weren't sure what they were being offered, although, it has to be said, some clients loved this fact about us.

CDs are non-bio-degradable. Design studios use large quantities of these silver discs. By throwing them into landfill sites, we are creating problems for our grandchildren. There are firms that will now take discarded CDs for various recycling purposes. Their addresses can be easily found on the internet. A recent report offered a note of optimism: 'Sanyo Electric has developed an optical disc based on a polymer derived from corn which, the company says, is as sturdy as current plastic discs but will biodegrade when disposed of.' Martyn Williams, *IDG News Service*, October 2003.

Here was an example of a creative philosophy combining with an ethical stance. By encouraging our designers to 'be themselves' we got striking and individualistic design, while simultaneously allowing designers to feel liberated and respected for what they did best. This notion of respect, and allowing each individual the maximum amount of freedom, extended to non-design staff. It was fundamental to the way we approached creative and business life and was woven into the fabric of the company.

There are, of course, other types of 'philosophy', and other types of ethics. Many designers believe in schools of design that come with inbuilt notions of ethical conduct. Modernism, for example, with its high moral tone of rationality and truthfulness; 'protest design', with its political and campaigning function; 'design for social good', with its rejection of purely financial motives in favor of design that benefits society. Others believe in sustainable design practices: 'green' issues such as the use of recycled materials for printing, and avoiding design that merely contributes to landfill sites, are increasingly preoccupying designers. I know designers who believe passionately in the democratizing and participatory merits of interactive digital design. And I know designers who carry a sword for aesthetic standards in design.

As well as having good people – and doing good work – studios need to have a philosophy; they need to have something they can believe in creatively, and they need to have an ethical base on which to operate as a business. I used to work for someone who told me that if the budget was poor, the client got poor service. If they paid for a day of my time, that was all they got, he said. I was young and inexperienced but I knew this philosophy was flawed. It might have the grim logic of the marketplace, but it wasn't a recipe for success. My creative philosophy has always been to do good work regardless of the budget. I tell myself there is no such thing as a bad job. This 'philosophy' has a shamelessly commercial aspect to it. It comes from a conviction that great work always gets noticed, and work that gets noticed leads to more and better assignments. In practice, it means that you have to do low-budget work with the same enthusiasm and commitment that you apply to big-budget work; this offends accountants and people like my former employer, but it is made easier by the fact that low-budget work is often more interesting than big-budget work, which usually comes with great dollops of pressure and angst.

I wrote earlier about the merits of giving designers (where appropriate) individual design credits. This is part of the same philosophy of encouraging authorship and acknowledging individual talent. In other words, the more each individual was allowed to be an individual, the stronger the group dynamic became. This notion was fundamental to the way we approached creative and business life and was woven into the fabric of the company.

Many designers have ethical prohibitions about working for tobacco companies or oil companies. Others have concerns over the role of the designer in modern society, which increasingly is one of unquestioning compliance with commercial culture. The writer Steven Heller investigates these issues in his book *Citizen Designer*. In his introduction he identifies one of the fundamental problems faced by all designers: 'Talented designers are predisposed to create good looking work. We are taught to marry type and image into pleasing and effective compositions that attract the eye and excite the senses. Do this well, we're told and good jobs are plentiful: do it poorly and we'll produce junk mail for the rest of our lives. However, to be what this book calls a "citizen designer" requires more than talent. As [Milton] Glaser notes, the key is to ask questions, for the answers will result in responsible decisions. Without responsibility, talent is too easily wasted on waste.'

There are countless ways in which we can, as designers, act responsibly: the way we treat our staff: the way we treat our clients; the way we treat our suppliers and collaborators; and the way we conduct ourselves as studios or individuals. Today, even big corporations are embracing ethical conduct through social responsibility charters. It is easy to be cynical about this development in corporate life, which only goes to demonstrate that we have to be genuine about our own efforts. And we have to be prepared to stand up for them and not discard them at the first opportunity. We have to believe in something and that something has to be genuine; and it has to be something by which we can be measured, firstly by ourselves and then by others. And we mustn't be frightened of promulgating our beliefs. People respect principles, especially in a world where they are becoming increasingly rare.

How to be a graphic designer, without losing your soul

Angela Lorenz

Angela Lorenz lives and works in Berlin. She had an unconventional design education, going straight from secondary school to professional life, where she received a thorough grounding in reproduction techniques, and acquired a mastery of digital technology. She has put this early training to good effect. She has evolved a highly distinctive 'digital aesthetic' which makes her work unique. Influenced by the possibilities of generative design and the techniques of digital-music production, Lorenz's output spans print design, screen design, programming and live visual presentations for electronic-music concerts. Lorenz works principally for a small community of electronic record labels, the most famous of which is the Berlin label Kitty-Yo. Although she is steadfastly independent and works alone, she is an enthusiastic collaborator, working on design projects with other designers and musicians from around the world.

www.alorenz.net

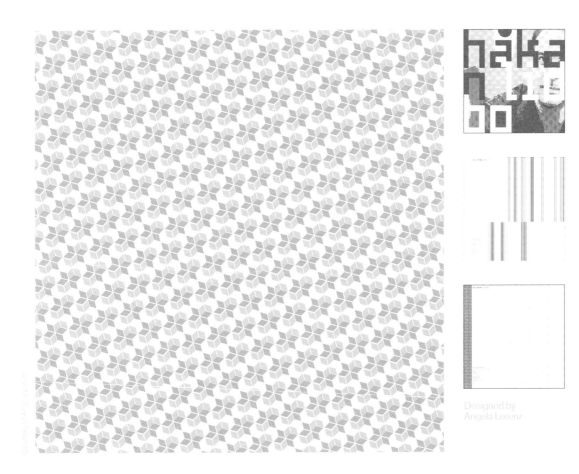

Designed by
Angela Lorenz

AL: When did you decide to become a designer? AL I don't think I had a very clear idea what that meant, or how to go about it in practice, until I basically was one. While I was still in school, I was fascinated with language, as a system or code, and particularly with written language; at the same time I knew I was good at art, but the idea of going to art school scared the hell out of me. So I guess I figured that the print industry might be somewhere in the middle and hence a good way to go – typesetting or printing just seemed more useful and reasonable to me than 'becoming a designer.'

All of this remained a bunch of vague ideas, though, until I was fifteen or sixteen: at that time, my school organized a short work internship for everyone, in an effort to put pupils in touch with the real world. Out of sheer luck, I ended up in a print shop, which was where I realized that it was actually practically possible to have fun with printing machines and repro cameras and earn a living at the same time. I don't actually remember doing any typesetting there, but I'm sure they did that, too. Anyhow, from then on I kept going in that direction: I took up a part-time job in phototypesetting, worked at a newspaper and finally started to work in pre-press; all that time I did freelance design jobs on the side as well, but it only evolved into a 'real' profession little by little.

You didn't go to art school. Can you talk about your design 'education'? I started to work at an experimental local paper, *Scheinschlag*, once I left school. That's where I learned a lot of basics in terms of technology and organization. I doubtless learned a lot about design in that time, too, but I wouldn't really call that an education; it was a mixture of learning by doing, reading up on things, and learning from others. I worked there for two years, and when I left I kept working with some of the people I had met there. We designed and produced another paper, posters, record sleeves, and I think I learned a lot in that time as well – I still remember how one of them called me one day just to let me know he'd figured out what alt-tab does in QuarkXPress.

At about the same time I took a part-time job in pre-press, which I kept for six years. The people there were very supportive, and I learned a lot of stuff that I would otherwise never have – from fixing postscript errors and wiring networks to tracking down how many kinds of Futura Ultra Bold there really are. All in all, I can't really tell where and when my 'education' ended and 'work' started – as for most 'self-taught' people, there probably isn't a clear dividing line.

Do you ever wish you'd had a formal education? Would your work be different if you'd had a formal design education? I'm not sure if my work would be so much different, but it would certainly look different. There's a lot of technology that I've never learned to use – I'm unable to draw a text typeface, I neither have the tools nor the knowledge to do lithographies or woodcuts or 8mm films, and my attempts at calligraphy are pretty ridiculous. On the other hand, I doubt there's many 'proper' designers who ever touched a litho press again after they graduated, so I'm not sure how big the practical difference really is. Also, I picked up a lot of things over time – from working in pre-press in particular – that I'd probably never have learned at college. Sometimes I wish I had a 'real' education, but that would be either computer sciences or civil law, definitely not design. If by some unlikely chain of events I had ended up in a design program, I'm sure I would only have hated it. It would have been fun for a while to be able to play with the nice toys, but apart from that I'm sure I would have been bored, unhappy, and a pain in the ass for everyone else.

You live and work in Berlin, but your work has no obvious sense of place. Can you talk about this? Why should it have an 'obvious sense of place'? I live here because my family moved here when I was a child – out of coincidence, that is. I don't have anything to do with it, and neither has my work. Call me a 'Berlin designer' if you want, but I find that about as meaningful as calling someone a 'vegetarian designer' (or is that the next trend, perhaps, now that 'female designers' are no longer an issue?). Seriously though, the music scene that I'm involved with – at least the interesting part of it, experimental electronic music – is simply not a local one. Quite the opposite. Nobody cares where people live as long as they answer their e-mails. The two most important collaborations I undertook in the last couple of years were with a designer in Belfast, and a musician in Saarbrücken. I would have a hard time to pin down where exactly the work 'took place' in either case. Inside a phone line, perhaps? And I actually do make a point of having the place (or places) where I worked on something listed in the credits. Maybe in 500 years it'll help someone to track down the development of electronic music in the ancient times that we live in.

Although you collaborate with musicians and occasionally with other designers, you chose to work alone. Why is this? Are you ever tempted to employ an assistant or start a studio? No studio for me, thanks. Right now I have just enough work to keep myself busy, and in case I get a job that's too much for one person there's plenty of other freelancers that I'd love to work with. I've had very good experiences so far with project-based collaborations, both short- and long-term ones, and if I look at the hassle that others have with their companies, I'm really happy that I don't have to deal with that. What's the point of a studio, anyway? Does the world really need another design company? Isn't the whole concept a bit overrated? To me it sometimes looks like the only benefit is that you get to pick a silly name and a 'head of' whatever on your business card. I don't even have a business card, so what would be in it for me?

You work in the electronic music scene, why is this? That's what I was interested in. Actually my main interest was (and still is) experimental music, not electronic music per se, but a lot of that has become electronic during the nineties. It's hard to pin down where and when it actually started, but over time it started to develop … musician A releases on label B, which in turn asks me to do something for C, who recommends me to D, and so on. I'm certainly happy that it turned out like this – even though it can be a bit one-sided sometimes, it's great to be able to work with people who do something that both client and designer really care about, and that's new to them as well as to me. It's on a whole different plane than yoghurt packaging, for example: you get to start from zero with every new release, there is no 'default look', and in music design you always have a task that's very clear and concrete. That's one of the things I really like about it – there is almost no waffling about 'target audiences' and such in experimental music; it's really about what's in the music.

How do you cope with the business side of being a designer? Did you have any business training? No. I'm lucky, though, because I have an incredibly good tax consultant. Fortunately, here in Germany it's not overly complicated to run a business as small as mine – as long as you don't earn too much and don't have any employees (or partners), it doesn't really count as a business at all, so the bookkeeping and such is relatively simple. Still, I don't know how I would have managed without professional help – when I first hired my tax consultant I know I was thinking his fee was rather high, but it's likely the best investment I ever made. Believe it or not, tax law can be an interesting subject if you have the right person explain it to you, and once you get the feeling that you roughly know what you're doing it can almost be fun.

Anyhow, I don't know how any amount of business training would have helped me in the harder cases that I encountered in the last couple of years – when a client goes bankrupt, they're bankrupt, and there's nothing you can do about it. Fortunately, the electronic music scene isn't very large, so most people tend to behave reasonably – most of the time I feel safe sticking with common sense.

Are you interested in working with bigger companies on bigger projects with bigger budgets? I wouldn't mind bigger budgets, of course, or big projects … but when it comes to big companies, from my limited experience there seems to be a correlation between size on the one hand and confusion, disinterest and boredom on the other. When I work for an individual or a small company, be it a musician or a painter or a shoemaker, they're usually very much into whatever it is they are doing, obviously, because it is their work. For someone who does marketing for brand X of company Y, this kind of interest would be rare.

What is the hardest thing about being a graphic designer and what is the best thing about being a graphic designer? 1. Doing a great job, but for the wrong person. 2. Refusing to work for someone, and realizing you were right.

There is more graphic design than ever before, and demand grows constantly. There are, it's true to say, occasional downturns in the economy that open up like unseen trapdoors just when we think we are doing well. These periodic economic dips mean that work for designers becomes scarce, and if our overheads are excessive, we can be damaged. But, when demand eventually returns, it is usually at an increased level. Everybody needs graphic design, or so it seems.

The world is literally 'covered in graphic design.' I'm writing these words in the Ardèche, a remote and rural district three hours from Lyons. All around me are hiking trails that lead into the foliage-covered hills. Remarkably, every path has a neatly designed sign that tells hikers where the path leads to and the distance to the next village. The signs are crisply printed, as good as you'd find in any shopping mall or airport, and designed by a professional graphic designer who has made them effective and attractive (Helvetica Rounded – friendly and legible). Even in the wilderness, it seems, we need graphic design.

Designed by Dieter Heil

Yet, despite the ubiquity of graphic design, designers rarely have enough work to enable them to feel comfortable, and even more rarely do they have enough of the right sort of work. It is common for design groups to have no idea what they will be doing in three or six months' time. Paradoxically, when we most need work, it always seems at its most scarce. The quest for new and better work is never-ending. As Dorothy Goslett notes: 'This will be the main battle of your whole … career: not only to find clients to start you going but constantly to be finding clients to keep you going. It is a battle which has to be waged more or less ceaselessly until you retire and one which will never allow you to rest on your laurels.'

But how well equipped are designers to find new work? We are rarely taught anything about the subject in design school, and few of us are given the training enjoyed by, for example, the bright-eyed photocopier sales executive who sold you that too-large, underused machine that sits in the corner of your studio, blinking malevolently. Fortunately, the training received by the photocopier salesman would not be much use to the designer, so we're not missing much. In fact, most modern sales strategies are next to useless in the design sphere. When it comes to finding new clients and winning new business for designers, cold calling, most forms of direct mail, and the ubiquitous e-mail spam are imprecise, intrusive and wasteful.

Selling design is not like selling other services, that would be too easy. Of course, it is perfectly possible to adopt the techniques used by the photocopier salesperson, but if you want to do meaningful work, then you have to 'sell' yourself with integrity and precision.

When clients choose a designer there is usually an element of subjectivity – of personal taste – in the selection process. For all but the most crass, appointing a designer, and commissioning design, is an act of personal commitment with strong emotional overtones. It could be argued that this is true of any service involving the hiring of an individual or a group of individuals: when we hire a plumber, for instance, we want someone who is efficient and who will work at a reasonable price – and we might choose a pleasant individual over an unpleasant one – but we don't base the decision on emotional factors. Mundane considerations concerning fees and production logistics all play a part in deciding whether to appoint a designer, but there is undeniably an element of personal taste and emotional commitment. There's a sense of design having something to do with the soul.

I had a client once who illustrated this point. He had commissioned me to produce a new identity for his company. When the work was completed he rang me to say that he was pleased with the outcome. He listed the various business benefits of the new identity, as he saw them, and then added: 'Anyway, what we've got now is good for the soul.' He wasn't an especially philosophical guy. He was just a clever businessman who could see a benefit in good design that couldn't be measured on the balance sheet.

But, despite recognizing the emotional and personal factors in selling design, we still have to find new work. Even when the economy is buoyant, this is never an easy job. It's especially difficult today when the buyer is nearly always king. As the business writers Jonas Ridderstrale and Kjelle Nordstrom state in their book *Funky Business:* 'In the surplus society the customer is more than king: the customer is the mother of all dictators. And this time it's for real. If the customer speaks you have to jump high and jump fast. The customer wants products in orange with purple spots. The customer wants them today in Fiji. You have to deliver otherwise you will soon be out of business.'

Big design firms have the funds to use all the latest sales and marketing strategies. They host seminars, give lectures, publish research, get written about in the business press rather than the design press (the sort of clients that the big design groups are after don't read the design press) and maintain ultra-slick websites. The rest of us have to rely on less sophisticated methods. We might have a studio brochure and a modest website. From time to time (usually when we run out of work) we send out e-mail newsletters, and every so often we send out an eye-catching mail-shot. We enter design competitions in the hope of being able to add the words 'award-winning' to a favorite piece of work. We submit projects to the design press in the expectation of attracting the camera-flash of media attention. And occasionally, we spruce up our portfolios and call existing or potential clients and ask them if we can show them our latest work – we usually only do this when we run out of work – in other words, when it's too late.

I was taken to task recently by a correspondent in the British journal *Design Week* for making disparaging remarks about 'conventional sales techniques' in the context of selling design. The writer said that although most sales practices had a bad reputation, if executed properly they could be successful. I have no objection to using traditional sales techniques: writing carefully worded letters, preparing targeted approaches to prospective clients can be effective if done properly. But to do them properly takes time and money and the sort of skills rarely possessed by the average graphic designer.

But regardless of our best efforts – sophisticated or not – a huge proportion of new business opportunities for designers are created in one of two ways: word of mouth, or random encounters in the business and social nexus that most of us live in. In other words, we get most of our work from people who've heard good things about us, and from networking with friends and associates.

Now, don't get me wrong here: I'm not advocating sitting about doing nothing and hoping that jobs will fly in through the window. They won't; you have to get up and open the window. You have to work incessantly to exploit every lead, connection and opportunity that comes your way. If you don't, you will struggle to have enough work to keep you busy, and you will eventually go bust. What I'm saying is that most traditional sales activities are close to worthless within the context of design and that you have to use other, more subtle methods. Quickhoney and eboy illustrator Peter Stemmler does a mailing of new work about twice a year, and yet most of his work comes from people he's worked with for a number of years; some people who have switched companies and taken Stemmler with them. Although most of Stemmler's work comes from people he knows, note that he still does promotional mail-outs. In truth, we have to do both: we must use every avenue (mailings, press coverage, awards) to get our work noticed, and we must look tirelessly for opportunities among the web of contacts and connections we have.

You know your new-business activity is working when potential clients start to call you. A call from a potential client with an invitation to meet, or, best of all, a nice project and a bit of cash to spend, is the goal of new-business activity. When you are doing all the calling, you are on the back foot. But how do we attract those calls? Well, by doing great work all the time; by acquiring, over time, a reputation as a talented studio or individual; and by shamelessly exploiting the chemistry of human relationships.

Dedicated new-business person

I've never met a designer with a studio who didn't want to find someone to help with the grind of finding new business. Unfortunately, good new-business people are rare, and so most designers have to do their own 'new business.' They are often good at it, much better than they think they are. It's just that it's a full-time job and, as a principal in a fledgling design firm, you also have to create design, not to mention perform countless administrative tasks. There are two sorts of new-business people. The first is the 'appointment setter.' He or she is usually a charming individual with a friendly manner, capable of intelligent and diligent research, and with the knack of persuading potential clients to agree to a meeting. The 'appointment setter' is often part-time, and might also perform other administrative functions within the studio.

The other sort of new-business person is a more recognizable beast. This is a confident individual who can get herself in front of people. There's really no better way to win work than through face-to-face meetings.

Of course, you have to be sure that the person representing your company is the sort of person you want to represent your company. And this is where it becomes difficult and why so many good design companies can't manage to find a new-business person. The principals of design companies invariably imagine that they are the only ones who can represent their company. But find the right person and it is perfectly possible to have someone represent your company effectively. If you get it right you will greatly increase the amount of work you generate. So it's a pretty good idea to find someone to help win new business. The first mistake that most people make is to put a new-business person on commission. Don't do this. If you pay someone commission they are going to be very unhappy when they bring you a project and you turn it down because it is not right for you or because you can't fit it into the schedule. Moreover, in their early days, new-business people can't be expected to do much beyond getting you onto pitch lists. This is fine: without the new-business person, you wouldn't be on the pitch list. But what happens if you pitch and don't win the job? Does the new-business person still expect commission? Of course not, yet they've done their job and they rightly expect a reward. After all, they didn't lose the pitch, you did.

A good new-business person needs to be part of the team, sharing the highs and lows of success and failure. They need to be part of your studio culture. They need to love design and they need to feel that their efforts are as important as those of the designers. They need to know that finding and winning new business is a creative act in itself. By all means, build in a reward or incentive system, but make sure it is similar to the reward and incentive schemes that you have for other staff. Any other system creates distortions and tensions that are irreconcilable to life in an intelligent design studio.

Which brings us to the second rule when employing a new-business person: don't assume that you need someone like our friend the photocopier salesman: you don't. You are selling ideas, not machines, so avoid hotshot salespeople, they are not what you want. 'Hotshot' salespeople think all jobs are good. This is not the case. A good new-business person will know which jobs are right and which are not. The ability to distinguish is the difference between a successful new-business person and one who is a failure.

But there's something else you can do; you can turn everyone in your company into a new-business person. Get everyone to add the words 'new business' to their job descriptions. Encourage people to think that no matter what their job is, they also have a business-generating role. Encourage people to realize that every gesture, every action, has a new-business consequence. It starts with the junior designers and runs all the way through to the directors. This sounds depressing: it sounds as if I'm advocating a company of pushy business-fixated automatons. Nothing could be further from the truth. What it means is that you acknowledge the fact that everything a designer does has an effect on their reputation, and consequently on their ability to attract clients. Even suppliers and professional advisers can be harnessed into performing an unwitting new-business role; treat them right and they become powerful advocates of your company. Then just sit back and wait for the phone to ring. The first call will be from someone selling photocopying machines, but the next one…

I was once called in to see a senior marketing director of a sports and leisure brand – a bona fide 'cool brand'; a household name. The man explained that he was looking for new companies to work with over the coming year, and he showed me the sort of projects they had coming up. It was one of the most depressing meetings I've ever attended. This 'cool brand' controlled every aspect of its communications and only employed designers to implement this neatly calculated 'coolness'. The possibility for genuine radical expression was zero. He didn't become a client.

2

Finding clients

Clients are everywhere, often where you least expect them to be. But it's a well-established rule of design that you rarely get to work with the clients you most want to work with. You can make a wishlist, and you can make heated overtures to the names on the list and, occasionally, you will be successful. But chances are your targets are everyone else's targets, and it is much wiser to look for clients off the beaten track. Most clients are found by accident or by tortuous paths that all lead back to luck and coincidence.

It's tempting to go after clients who already exhibit good design sense. But think about it: if they are known for good design, it will almost certainly mean that they are knowledgeable about design; that they will know who the good designers are; that they will know how to commission design – a rarity; and that they will gravitate towards the best studios. If you are among the 'best', don't worry, they will find you. If you're not yet in the upper echelons of design stardom, perhaps you are wasting your time chasing them. Better instead to go after companies and institutions that need real root-and-branch help. With these clients, you will have to work harder, but the results, if you are successful, will be infinitely more satisfying. There is more personal satisfaction in taking a client with no apparent potential and producing effective and resonant work for them than there is in working for so-called 'cool brands'.2

For the contemporary graphic designer, finding clients means finding and taking part in pitches. They are unavoidable (paid and unpaid), but they are often the only way to break into new areas. If you are going to take part in a pitch you have to be prepared to devote countless hours to ensure your presentation is impeccable. It's the only way. Pitches have to be executed as well as finished projects are. Many public-sector pitch lists (it's called tendering) are published on the Internet. You will have to look hard to find them. Don't confuse design projects with invitations to supply latrines to the Hungarian army – you may find that your studio is not best suited to this task. But keep looking: they are there.

No matter how busy you are, start a database of contacts – actual and desired. There are various proprietary databases that you can buy – a good IT person will be able to recommend a suitable one. But, even if you have to write down the information in a notebook, log the name and contact details of everyone you meet and come into contact with. No matter how tenuous the connection, log their details. You probably know more people who commission design than you think. Write down a list of everyone you know. Someone on that list will commission design, or perhaps works for a company that commissions design. Scan magazines looking for suitable names and companies. Read the job vacancy pages in newspapers: if you see a vacancy for someone, perhaps a marketing director, to 'oversee the company's image', then you know that in a couple of months' time there will be a new person trying to make a mark, perhaps looking for bright new talent to help him or her do it.

Do all this, and in a remarkably short space of time you will accumulate a database of contacts. These are the future recipients of your ongoing promotional activities. You need to love this list. Look at it constantly. Tend it carefully. Make sure it is up to date. If you're unsure about a name on the list, check it. It looks shabby if you contact a person who left a post a year before: it shows you're behind the beat. When your list is ready, you need to feed it with seductive and alluring material. You need to send them something beautiful.

Here's a little pearl of wisdom someone told me about: when you write a letter, especially a letter promoting you or your company, always write the address on the envelope by hand. It is so rare to get a letter with a handwritten address that most people instinctively open these first. Perhaps we think we are getting a letter from a friend, or someone who knows us. Nevertheless, when confronted with a pile of letters, the one with the handwritten address is the one we open first. (It helps if you've got good handwriting – most designers have – but if you haven't, get someone with good handwriting to address the envelope for you.)

Promotional tools

Your work, and the reputation it generates, is your most valuable promotional tool. In a later chapter we will look at how you get your work noticed: if it's good enough it will be noticed without much effort on your part. It is one of the happier aspects of today's sophisticated design scene that opportunities to gain recognition have greatly increased. In fact, you need do nothing beyond great work, confident in the knowledge that, if it is genuinely good, it will be spotted. But it would be a brave studio that did nothing to promote itself; in reality this is a never-ending activity and everyone has to do it.

The primary tools of communication and promotion for a studio are its identity (as it appears on stationery, website, etc.), a portfolio, a website and printed literature (which typically might include direct mail, flyers, e-mail flyers, posters and postcards). And this is before we even get to the most effective and potent tool at your disposal: word of mouth.

The portfolio

I've already discussed the portfolio in relation to a designer seeking employment in a design studio, but creating a company portfolio to show to potential clients is a different kettle of eels. When a designer shows a portfolio to a prospective employer (usually another designer), they are demonstrating their understanding of the subject of design. When a design studio is showing a portfolio of its work to a prospective client, they are demonstrating their understanding of communication, business and, probably, life itself.

Portfolios are emotive things. Designers are never happy with them. I've known many competent and talented designers who've begun portfolio sessions with an apology: 'I'm just about to redo it,' they say; or, 'Sorry, it's a bit out of date.' It seems to be a designer foible that the portfolio is 'never finished,' and never 'representative of current work.' Yet far from being a sign of weakness, this is a good sign: it indicates a restless and necessary desire to improve and develop. When someone tells you their portfolio is great, the only suitable response is to leave the room. The correct relationship between a designer and his or her portfolio is one of constant doubt and questioning.

As designers, objectivity about our work is hard to achieve, and as a consequence, designers are not very good at putting their own portfolios together. I have a rule that I never let designers get involved in the making of a studio portfolio. I am ruthless and dispassionate about what work is included, and how it is presented. I base my decisions on responses and feedback I get from clients, and old-fashioned intuition. This means that many favorite pieces get left out. I show my efforts to the individual designers concerned, but I rarely listen to their views about what is missing.

Now, I have a confession to make: I never once opened up a portfolio in front of a client without feeling a sharp sense of its inadequacy. I suspect most designers – even confident and successful ones – feel this similarly at the moment of testing. You would think that it is a dangerous sensation to experience, as you are about to make an important presentation. It is, yet it is also what carries me through the presentation. It always makes me work harder and forces me to make an adrenalin-charged presentation. Of course, if the presentation goes well, then I look at the portfolio as if it is the finest thing since Leonardo da Vinci's sketchbooks. This warm glow lasts only until the next presentation I'm required to make.

Portfolios – the actual receptacle you carry your work in – needn't be the black, zipper folders that designers traditionally use to display their work to potential clients. Today, you can have a portfolio on a laptop, a CD, a video cassette. You can have your portfolio online. I even had a guy turn up recently with all his work on an iPod. But if you are still attached to the black zipper case at least consider loose sheets rather than bound ones. These can be handed round (you often have to present to more than one person), and they avoid the tortuous process of clipping and unclipping sheets.

A digital projector hooked up to your laptop is a sexy and effective way to show work. The image is projected onto a wall (preferably white), and everyone faces the screen. If you are uncomfortable standing and facing a roomful of people, then standing at the back of the room as your audience faces the screen is a less challenging alternative. In a darkened room (some projectors work in daylight) it is possible to create an intimate and intensely focused experience. If the work is arranged around a menu, you can select your work according to the needs of your audience: if an interest in identity arises, for instance, you can cut straight to examples.

And since your work is run off a laptop, it also means that you can store all your work as digital files. With a traditional 'paper' portfolio, it is rarely possible to accommodate all your work; and I've never made a presentation where I haven't regretted the absence of a particular piece of work.

So, what do you show? The answer to this will depend on what sort of work you do. If you are a book designer, you might want to show spreads from the books you've done, as digital files as well as a physical copy of the book itself. If you are a web designer, you might want to show frames from the sites you've built, and you might want to show sites stored on the hard drive of your laptop or even visit them online. But regardless of what you show, and how you show it, you need to show your work in context: the narrative history of your work is what clients want to see – not just a succession of arresting images.

To do this, try and show your work (where appropriate) in situ. By this I mean, if, for example, you have designed a logo that was subsequently used by an advertising agency on billboards or in television commercials, show an image of the billboard or a frame from the commercial. You will probably dislike the way the advertising agency has designed the billboard, and the TV commercial might be cheesy, but your client almost certainly won't share your squeamishness. What I'm saying here is that it's not enough, as it was when you were looking for a job as a designer, to merely show your work, now you need to show your work *working*. This is the secret of a good portfolio.

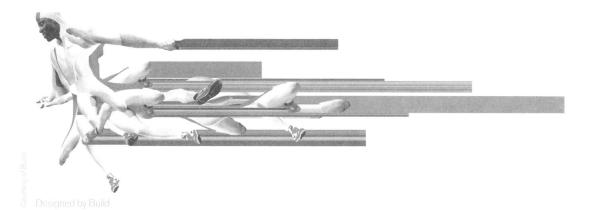

Courtesy of Build

Designed by Build

Website

If you thought creating your studio identity was hard work, wait until you come to do the studio website. Before you start, spend some time looking at the sites of other design studios. I say this not in the hope that you will accumulate ideas – quite the opposite. I say it so that you will know what *not* to do. Most design company websites are woeful. They all look the same, and they say the same trite things. These sites make the mistake, like young designers attending a first client meeting, of talking about themselves too much. On their websites, designers can reveal such staggering depths of self-absorption that if they were to do the same at a social gathering they'd clear the room in seconds. My advice is – keep it simple and shut up about yourself.

You have a choice to make. You can either make a site that dazzles by its sheer brilliance: in other words go for a sensory experience that attracts visitors like moths round a light, or you can make a site that contains a measured and carefully modulated description of who you are and what you do. It is sometimes possible to do both, but both approaches require different skills and it's rare to find them combined in a small company.

Regardless of which route you choose, think carefully about the language you use and the visual statements you make. Don't assume that your audience is waiting with barely contained anticipation to respond to your invitation. Very few clients trawl through websites looking for suitable designers. Typically, clients visit websites after a designer has been recommended to them, or if they have been directed there by your own promotional efforts. They go to the site looking for additional information. Bear this in mind when you are creating your site. The key to a good website is the first page you see. Because of search engines, visitors will rarely enter a site through your home page, so every page needs to carry information that enables visitors to contact you. It can be made into an attractive detail that will appeal to a smart potential client.

Every page should also carry a menu that enables a visitor to find out who you are, what you do and a list of your clients. It depresses me to see the importance potential clients place on a designer's client list. So many of them seem to need the endorsement that comes from seeing a well-stacked client list. I live in hope that a new breed of enlightened client will emerge who doesn't need this endorsement: a breed that relishes the fact that they 'got there first'.

Promotional literature

I was once part of an awards jury that looked at the brochures of various design groups. The entrants had worked hard to make their promotional literature effective and compelling: they might as well have sent out bags of cold custard. The results were uniformly depressing. Even the mildly controversial ones ('branding is dead'; 'this is not a sales brochure') were formulaic and spirit sapping. This made me think how depressing it must be to be a client and to be deluged with design company literature. Over the years, I've produced my fair share of this stuff ('… is a multidisciplinary design group with an innovative approach to …'): my only defense is that I didn't enter any of it into design competitions; I knew it was rubbish.

What do you do to avoid looking and sounding like everyone else? How do you find a fresh arrangement of words that inspires rather than deflates the reader? In the self-promotion chapter I'll look more closely at how to create effective promotional material. But for now, let's be clear about why you must produce printed or electronic promotional items: you must do so to attract attention. Even then, it is unrealistic to expect to be hired directly from your promotional material – responses to direct mail and promotional devices are notoriously poor. Now, this doesn't mean that you don't do them, but you must avoid sending second-rate material; it will only join all the other promotional detritus that pours through everyone's mailbox in the trash. And direct mails on their own are rarely enough, you have to follow them up with phone calls.

The effect of sending out promotional literature is cumulative. We've all heard stories about clients who received something in the post from a design company and rang up immediately with an offer of work. It happens, but it's rare. A more likely (though also rare) outcome is that after receiving two or three striking items via e-mail, and after receiving a friendly call from you to ask if the document has arrived and if it is of any interest, a client might invite you to attend a meeting or join a pitch list.

In truth, what more often happens is clients who receive frequent offerings from designers file them in an ever-thickening file and forget about them, or, worse, simply throw away what they are sent.

I've noticed that a lot of good designers don't bother with any sort of promotional literature. They rely on their work to generate interest, and they rely on other people writing about them. To have a sharp-eyed journalist analyze your work in a good design magazine is preferable – and more convincing – than doing it yourself in an expensive and time-consuming brochure. But until you have earned it, persuading journalists and editors that you are a suitable subject for their attention will be difficult.

Until then, and while you are still drumming up business for your new studio, it is desirable to have an item of printed literature to send out, and to leave with potential clients. You might start with postcards. On one side you can show an arresting image, on the other you need only have the barest information – project name, client name and your contact details. You might want to next consider direct mail, flyers, e-mail flyers, posters, etc. The same rules apply. Avoid clichés and avoid the obvious. Make your promotional activities distinctive and daring; force your personality into whatever you do. Otherwise, like the pizza-flyers you get in your mailbox, it simply won't get noticed.

Courtesy of Karlssonwilker

Designed by
Karlssonwilker

Alexander Gelman

Alexander Gelman is president and a founding partner of Design Machine, a leading brand consultancy based in New York, whose clients include Absolut Vodka, Apple, Chanel, HBO, IBM, MTV, Sony and United Airlines. Gelman is president of the US chapter of Alliance Graphique Internationale (AGI) and a member of its international executive committee. He was a design fellow in 2003/04 at MIT's Media Laboratory. He served as a board member on the Design Advisory Committee of the Cooper-Hewitt National Design Museum and on the executive board of The Art Directors Club, New York. Gelman taught visual communication and design at Parsons Institute of Design, the School of Visual Arts, Cooper Union, and Yale University. His work is in the collections of the Museum of Modern Art and the Cooper-Hewitt National Design Museum.

www.designmachine.com

Designed by
Alexander Gelman

You trained in Moscow: what did you get from studying in Russia that you wouldn't have got elsewhere? AG A bunch of useless skills … like distilling vodka or making cardboard out of paper.

You have strict guidelines for qualification as a Design Machine client. I've never seen this before. Is it good for business? It's good for personal sanity.

Your philosophy of 'subtraction' is well known. How important is it for a contemporary design group to have a philosophy? It's good to believe in something and have standards, but philosophy is not something you can cultivate.

How does teaching feed into your work? It adds extra stress, but it also trains me to communicate ideas more clearly, and stimulates thinking (free of a client's internal politics).

What do you think about the current generation of students? They're just as good as any other generation.

What are the key attributes the modern designer needs? Friends and money.

How do you attract new clients to Design Machine? I don't. When a potential client somehow shows up I do all I can to discourage them from hiring us. They usually end up hiring Pentagram.

What do you say to young designers starting out today? Don't be afraid to try things. The worst that can happen is that you'll get fired, which could turn out to be the best thing after all.

Andy Cruz

Andy Cruz founded the design firm and digital-type foundry House Industries in Wilmington, Delaware, in 1993 with partner Rich Roat. From their early experiments with distressed digital type to their more recent Neutraface (created in consultation with architect Richard Neutra's son, Dion), they have pioneered a style of working that requires high levels of creativity and entrepreneurialism. Although they dislike the term 'retro', it's Cruz's and Roat's clever reworking of early-sixties visual culture – everything from high Modernism to Ed 'Big Daddy' Roth's muscle cars – that distinguishes their work. The Delaware-based firm celebrated its tenth birthday with the publication of a sumptuous eponymous book, which itself is a polished example of the House Industries design ethos: overprinted finishes, washes and metallic inks. The tone is set right from the start: 'Book completely overdesigned and profusely illustrated by House Industries'.

www.houseindustries.com

Neutra Boomerang chair
by House Industries

AS Can you tell me how you became a designer? AC I loved to draw as a kid. Skateboarding and punk rock helped connect the dots.

What was your college experience like? Very nice … I didn't go.

Was there something that you learned in school that you only now appreciate? I attended a vocational and trade high school that had a traditional commercial art program: lettering, paste-up, etc. I bitched about comping Helvetica and Times on vellum when you could typeset anything on the (then-almighty) Mac Plus we had in the classroom. It took me a while to figure out any monkey can select fonts on the computer … drawing type is something I wish I spent more time on.

You seem to represent a new entrepreneurial trend in design. House Industries does so many things besides commercial projects. Can you talk about this? It started with our fonts. We found that most design clients are a pain in the ass. Rich Roat (my partner) and I decided we needed a product rather than a service and House Fonts was born. Since then we've tried to develop House products that escape the make-believe world of graphic design and cross over to the mainstream. Most recently we've started a House clothing line and opened a store in London to put our work to the test.

How do you attract attention to House Industries? Meticulous attention to detail, ridiculous self-portraits and plenty of overprinted metallic inks.

How did you learn to be a businessman as well as a designer? Fortunately, Rich is the business end of House. I just have to try and make things look interesting … doesn't always work.

What more could art schools do to equip students for working life? Make all the high-concept graphic design students become painting or sculpture majors. There's plenty of design done for other graphic designers, and I have a feeling this starts at the art-school level. I'd like to see kids who study graphic design learn how to push a pencil or a brush more than a mouse. A better blend of fundamental skills with whatever computer tricknology kids need to get jobs these days might result in a better visual landscape than the one we've got to look at these days.

Do you have a design philosophy? Do your thing. Sure, you're gonna take on some shitty jobs that pay the bills, but if you're true to what you want to do (and not so much to what the client wants you to rip off) you'll feel much better about going to work. Not to sound all 'dad' about it, but if you're lucky, people will eventually pay you to do what you enjoy.

A lot of students I meet say they have to move to the cities to do good work. Yet you've proven that you can be successful by not moving to one of the world's great capitals. Can you talk about this? If you can get a Fed Ex truck to your front door it doesn't matter where you are. Making the scene is always fun, but we've found we can get more work done without big city distractions.

What is your view of the current design scene? I think graphic designers are mistaking the words 'design annual' for 'style guide'.

Designed
by House Industries

I love clients, even the bad ones. In fact, I prefer 'difficult' clients to 'easy' clients. It feels like cheating to have a client who approves all your ideas and never questions what you are doing. I like a fight, and I get satisfaction from winning over a difficult client. Of course, I don't always win, and, like every other designer, I've encountered my share of arrogant know-it-alls who don't want to listen to any advice whatsoever, and who want to control the design process from start to finish. But I've had more successes than failures, and total defeat is rare. It's rare because I never allow myself to forget that designer and client are locked into a marriage that, like a real marriage, has to be an equal partnership if it is to last and produce any worthwhile offspring.

In 1956, the great Russian-born designer Misha Black delivered a paper to the Sixth International Design Conference in Aspen, Colorado called 'The Designer and the Client.' Black co-founded Design Research Unit, one of the first design consultancies, and he is one of the few designers to comment insightfully on the relationship between the designer and the client. His observations are as relevant today as they were in the fifties. Black said: 'I am not suggesting that the influence of the client is necessarily harmful. The opposite is often true. When the client and the designer are in sympathy, they can together produce better work than that of which either alone would be capable.'

Taken from the paper 'The Designer and the Client.' Reprinted in Looking Closer 3: Critical Writings on Graphic Design (New York: Allworth Press), 1999.

Without clients there is no graphic design and without demanding clients there is no great graphic design. Yet, the poor old client is often airbrushed out of design history and design journalism, not to mention critical and theoretical discourse. Clients are usually cited, if at all, as an amorphous, barely tolerated and reactionary force. They are rarely interviewed, and it is unusual for them to be congratulated on their sponsorship, patronage or encouragement of good design. The design writer Robin Kinross, writing about Dutch designer Karel Martens, in *Eye* magazine, even went as far as to turn his nose up at the word 'client': '*opdrachtgevers* [commission giver], the Dutch word is better than our sleazy "client,"' he notes. And you know exactly what he means.

But you must resist these demonizing tendencies in dealing with your 'commission givers,' it's counterproductive. And despite talk of 'educating clients' and 'finding enlightened clients,' whether you like it or not the onus is on you – the designer – to change, not the client. If we want clients to listen to us and respect us, we have to deal with them with the utmost sensitivity and respect. This chapter speaks up for the client. Even the bad ones.

It is often said by disgruntled designers that 'so and so' (here they usually name a famous designer) has been successful because he or she had an indulgent client. This remark is sometimes true, although it is often flavored with a splash of envy. There are indeed exceptional clients who act more like patrons than clients. But they are rare. In reality, even the exceptional clients have to be won over and tirelessly cajoled into supporting and commissioning our ideas rather than following the fuzzy notions they have about how design should be done.

Take Neville Brody's epoch-defining work for the British magazine *The Face*. Brody approached the editor Nick Logan about doing some layouts for the magazine. Logan made him wait nine months before allowing him to do a few spreads. Brody used this hard-won opportunity to impress Logan, who then famously hired him to design the magazine and the results became part of graphic design history. My point here is that Brody earned his success. It wasn't handed to him on a plate by a super-indulgent client in a bravura gesture of largesse.

Treat your clients like you treat your friends. This is not saying make your clients into friends; just treat them like friends. A certain cool detachment is recommended, although it is perfectly fine to have friends as clients, and indeed it is quite common to have clients who, over time, become friends. But there is much to be said for keeping a barrier between intimacy and professional matters. Nevertheless, just as we have to work at friendships, which can be destroyed by a casual remark or a selfish action, so we also have to work at maintaining client relationships. And to make matters more difficult, no two clients are the same. They all need something different – this one needs lots of attention, this one is obsessed with value for money, this one is suspicious of designers and unconvinced by arguments about the value of good design. Designers have to be hyper-attentive to the individual needs of clients. Finding out what they want from you – from design – is the first task of the designer. Assuming that they all want the same thing, and assuming that they all want what you want, is dangerously short-sighted.

The Face
designed by Neville Brody

This is not to say that clients are always right, or that you should do everything they say. Clients need to be challenged when they are wrong, and by not challenging them we are doing them a professional disservice. As John Warwicker, one of the founders of Tomato, says elsewhere in this book: 'Tell your clients when they are wrong.' Warwicker is a charismatic and articulate man with a glittering track record. Most clients *will* listen to him; he's earned the right to dish out the occasional reprimand. But for the young designer with no track record to flaunt, a more mollifying approach is advisable.

Misha Black notes what happens when the relationship between designer and client becomes skewed: 'In the second-class design office, where expediency controls honesty, the influence of the client is decisive. No more time is spent on the job than the minimum necessary to satisfy the client, and if the client is incapable of judging between a solution that is properly resolved and one that is only partially resolved, then it is the latter he receives. This is the path of mediocrity, to the rapid deterioration of standards, and, for the designer, to an insistent sense of dissatisfaction not compensated by the increasing bank balance that often results from a willingness to produce shoddy work.' Black's observation cuts to the heart of the matter. The relationship must be one of equals.

The question I am most commonly asked by young designers is: 'How can I stop clients making changes to my work?' There is, alas, no easy answer to this. And of course, if your work is flawed, ill-conceived or poorly executed, then you deserve to have it changed. The only way to avoid clients interfering with good work is to establish a proper working relationship at the outset. It is no good trying to establish working practices further down the line when you hit trouble: by then it's too late. And I don't mean handing your client a list of demands and conditions: I'm talking about establishing the framework for a mature working relationship (as described in chapter two) where you listen and absorb the client's point of view, but where you conduct yourself in such a way that your client is inclined to allow you to have a point of view.

The 'battle' (I'm loath to use such a confrontational word, but there is no other term that better emphasizes the importance of this) must start at the outset. Unless you establish at the first meeting the working patterns by which you intend to execute the project, you will find it difficult to assert yourself later in the relationship. Of course, it is always possible to win over clients at any time in the design process, but the later you leave it the more difficult it becomes to tell your client that you don't want to include the logo her school-age daughter has designed and which she has suggested you use. (This happened to me.)

If a client says to you, 'I'd like you to incorporate this logo that someone did for me,' you can say, 'Okay, it will fit in very well' or you can say 'Okay,' and then seethe internally at its utter inappropriateness. Or, you can take the logo and say, 'I'm happy to try it, but I'd like to show you some alternative ideas I have in mind.' Most clients will find this suggestion reasonable and acceptable. If they don't, perhaps you should start to worry. All you've done is try to establish a mature relationship that cuts both ways.

In an interview with the design writer Rick Poynor, Ian Anderson of Designers Republic described the way he approaches a project: 'The way we perceive working with clients,' notes Anderson, 'is that what they provide is the puzzle that needs to be solved. We are happier without too much creative input from the client because, for us it is a little like someone leaning over your shoulder and doing the crossword for you. We want them to set us the challenge and then, as artists, we want to go back to them and for them to say "That is fantastic. That is more than we ever could have imagined."' Anderson's crossword metaphor is good. Most clients would understand what he means. And by having a philosophy of dealing with clients, Anderson can define his working methodologies. Of course, some clients will reject this – they will seek to impose their control. Then you have a choice: you can give in and take the money, or you can walk away. But you can also negotiate an acceptable outcome by accommodating the client's wishes wherever possible. The one thing you can't do is win every battle. Life as a designer isn't like that. But if you don't have a formula, you are at the mercy of their every whim.

Designers must also have the modesty and self-critical skills to know when they are wrong. I've been pulled up by clients for conceptual errors, or mistakes in execution, and when I've recovered from the blow of being corrected I've realized that I have been guilty of overconfidence or arrogance. As designers, we are not always right, and we have no monopoly on wisdom – although some designers think they do. We are capable of many crimes against common sense in the pursuit of our 'vision,' and while we must be quick to defend our work, we must be equally quick to admit when we are wrong. Nothing flags a designer's second-rate status more clearly than the conviction that he or she is never wrong.

Only marginally more heinous than telling a client that you are perfect is telling a client what they should think about the work you are showing them. It is a great temptation to do this. As designers, we want to establish our omnipotence. We know what we'd like our clients to think about our work. But we must resist the temptation to tell them what to think, or how they should be responding to our work. This aggravates clients and denies them the free role that we, as designers, expect to enjoy ourselves. Telling a client what to think about work is the equivalent of a client telling a designer how to design. You must, therefore, always allow clients to come to their own conclusions before you do or say anything. Then, and only then, if they don't share your view, and if you are sure that you are right, you can argue your case. But remember to do it from the audience's perspective, not your perspective.

Time is also essential in allowing clients to formulate a response. Never demand an immediate response. Encourage your client to 'think about it,' before giving you a definitive response. Think about it: you've had weeks, perhaps months, to devise this work, you've had time to look at it from different angles, you might even have shown it around and received some helpful comments, but the poor client has to make up his or her mind on the spot. This is unrealistic. I've often had a poor reaction to an initial presentation of work, but after encouraging my client to take more time before coming to a final conclusion, I've had the verdict overturned. It doesn't always happen, but it's worth trying if you don't get a favorable response the first time round. It is also advisable to insist on a period of consideration if you are presenting to multiple decision makers. In this situation, individuals will feel the need to make snap judgments so as to assert their independence; others will avoid saying what they really feel out of fear or uncertainty.

Now, I know what you are thinking: that graphic design is usually *supposed* to work first time round – there are no second chances with a poster or a web banner. Commercial imperatives demand that these and other pieces of graphic communication work from the get-go. But the 'presentation' situation is artificial. No-one is looking at your work with genuinely objective eyes: everyone is trying to second-guess the intended audience's reaction. Time will help introduce a note of objectivity.

I'd be failing in my duty here if I didn't stress the importance of personality in all this. Designers tend to be either heroes or doormats. If you are a doormat, then I'm afraid you will, on occasions, be stepped on. If, on the other hand, you are a hero – but a kindly and listening hero, with only your client's interests at heart – you will find yourself less trampled on. How you acquire hero-like status is a matter of personal odyssey and psychological discovery. Most heroes seem to be born with it, but you can also acquire it: it comes slowly and it comes as a consequence of how you learn from the knock-downs and set-backs we all encounter as designers. I've seen designers acquire it over time, and it's a beautiful thing to witness.

2   Bad or ineffective clients are usually poor at seeing things through the eyes of their audience. They are often businesspeople who are required to make assumptions about their audience, and they can get these assumptions wrong, just like anyone else. The amount of knowledge and insight a designer brings to the definition of an audience is critical.

I'm always suspicious of designers who blame everything on their clients. What they're doing is blaming their own shortcomings as designers on their clients. I'm often told by new (and not so new) designers that they don't get offered interesting jobs. Yet when I look at the projects they've worked on, the assertion rarely stands up. There is no such thing as a bad job, and the responsibility for a successful outcome rests firmly on the shoulders of the designer. Of course, it is true to say that designers occasionally find themselves in impossible situations, trapped in projects where they are powerless to act and where they are reduced to slave labor. But in most cases, the eventual outcome of any project is in the hands of the designer. Failure to accept this leads to unhappiness and mediocre work.

Keeping clients

Once you've got a client, and once you've adapted to his or her ways of working, and once you've evolved a relationship that makes working with them rewarding both creatively and financially, it's worth hanging on to them. Retaining a client is easier than finding a new one. And it's worth remembering that the most difficult job you will ever do for a client is the first one you do for them.

Designers forget this in their rush to chalk up an instant hit. In doing a first job for a new client, the designer encounters problems that simply won't be problems second time round. Yet this doesn't stop impatient designers condemning a client as irredeemably bad, when it is merely a case of 'first job syndrome.' The smart designer talks to his or her client about the problems in a frank and open manner. Explore ways of resolving these questions in the future. If you demonstrate a willingness to change and adapt (without losing your integrity) your client will bend accordingly. If not, perhaps they are not worth hanging on to.

Repeat business is highly desirable, but you mustn't suppose it will happen automatically without effort on your behalf. You have to tell your client that you are available and willing for more work. I've never been a fan of client entertainment, but at the end of a successful project a client lunch can often be a good way to cement a relationship, and provide a platform for a discussion about your working relationship. Get your client to come to your studio and have a catered lunch. This sends out a better signal than taking him or her to a posh restaurant. And it's cheaper.

Developing clients

In the modern business world, long-term relationships with clients are an increasing rarity. Contemporary business thinking states that businesspeople need to keep their suppliers on their toes by chopping and changing them constantly. There is a brutal marketplace logic in this, but it is not necessarily the way for clients to get the best out of designers, where long-term relationships often lead to a deeper understanding of a client's objectives, and more focused work. However, vigilance is necessary. Look for signs of complacency or patterns of formulaic behavior in yourself and your studio. Be tough with yourself, or your client will do it for you.

Wherever possible, it is worth devoting time and energy to developing clients. What does this mean in practice? It means taking an interest in their affairs, and it means showing initiative. It means keeping a line of communication open so that they are able to share their thinking and their plans with you. Regular communication should mean just that, and should not mean pestering. For example, if you hire a new member of staff with a new set of skills or win some new business in a relevant sector, tell your other clients about it. If you come across some interesting information or market intelligence relevant to your client, let them know about it. In the gaps between big projects, if your client needs you to do smaller jobs, such as design invitations or other small items,₃ do this work with the same relish that you reserve for the bigger projects, and use it as an invaluable opportunity to keep lines of communication open. In the chapter devoted to self-promotion, we'll look at ways you can keep clients abreast of your work and achievements.

Clients sometimes 'go quiet' because they have run out of budget. Perhaps they are waiting for next year's budget to be allocated. If so, small jobs like invitations can sometimes be done at no charge (or at cost) if you are confident that a client will appreciate this gesture, and return the favor when
3   budgets are available.

One last thought: I've often found that even quite smart clients are mystified by how designers and design groups operate. We think they know, but they rarely do. So it can be surprisingly helpful if you let clients know how you operate: tell them who does what, and why they do what they do. This simple act of demystification can improve the way clients regard you, and improve your working relationship.

Sacking clients

We've talked a great deal about finding, developing and clinging on to clients: sometimes though, you have to dump them. There are some clients who are frankly exploitative and who can cause damage to you and your company. If you have to sack a client, make sure there are no loose ends. Have you delivered everything you are obliged to give them? Do they owe you any money? Are there any other links that can't be easily severed? If you are satisfied on all these points, and once you've established that the client is worthless, sack them.

There are other sorts of clients worth ditching: time-wasters and con artists. Believe me, they exist. In the design world, they are perhaps not as plentiful as they are in other fields, but they are out there. You need to develop a sixth sense to spot these people. I've encountered many time-wasters, and one out-and-out con-man. Both breeds are easy to spot. They rarely put anything in writing, they don't let you visit them, and they run away if you ask for references.

But it is not only the unpleasant clients you need to ditch. I've had delightful, well-meaning clients, who, despite their good intentions, have been unable to pay their bills. When you discover that a client can't pay their bills stop working for them immediately. Don't rack up any more costs on their behalf; put them on hold (no more work) until the matter is resolved. If it can't be resolved, you might need your lawyer on the case – but don't exacerbate the situation by carrying on working for someone who can't pay their bills.

Monopolized by clients

As you become better at finding new clients, better at looking after them, and better at retaining them, you encounter a new problem: over-reliance. Avoiding becoming reliant on a single client who accounts for too big a percentage of your business is a serious problem. An accountant will advise you on safe percentages, but don't allow a single client to dominate your business. You've put all your energy into servicing that client and in doing so you've forgotten to add new clients to your client list. You are at your most vulnerable when a client monopolizes you. If they leave, you will be stranded with the problem of replacing them.

With typical contrariness ex-Talking Heads singer David Byrne uses PowerPoint to create art. He has produced a book *E.E.E.I (Envisioning Emotional Epistemological Information)* with a DVD containing five PowerPoint presentations accompanied by original music. The book contains exploratory texts and graphic images created with the help of PowerPoint's built-in tools and visuals. Byrne appropriates a familiar corporate tool and makes something striking and witty with it.

The presentation

Presenting to clients is the ultimate test of the designer's communication skills. It is the moment of truth: the moment where we reveal our soul (or at least it's the moment where we find out if we are going to have some income in the weeks and months ahead). Many designers find it daunting to stand up before a roomful of people and present their work, and the first half-dozen or so times you do it, it is indeed daunting. But no-one expects designers to be orators. So it's okay to be nervous, and it is acceptable to be awkward, just so long as your work is good. I see designers getting into hopeless muddles because they are trying to be slick. Don't be slick, if you are a raw and rough-edged person. Be raw and rough-edged, but be yourself and be passionate. When I first started speaking to clients, and to other designers at conferences, I was sick with nerves. But I kept doing it, and gradually it became easier. Eventually it became, if not exactly stress-free, then at least much less of an ordeal. You just have to keep doing it.

Here's another piece of undying wisdom: the key to a successful presentation is not using PowerPoint. Never use PowerPoint. Your client will have had a PowerPoint presentation from a prospective IT supplier – or someone selling health insurance – just a few days prior to you turning up with your presentation. Unless you want to look like an IT supplier, don't use PowerPoint.

The other factor in good presenting is preparation. If you haven't organized every aspect of the presentation, don't bother turning up. Leave nothing to chance. It is especially important that you consider the order in which you show things. Take your audience on a simple step-by-step journey from beginning to end. Don't make assumptions, spell everything out. Begin by reiterating the brief, itemize your thinking, show your conclusions and end with a concise summary.

The great immutable law of making a design presentation is this: tell your audience what you are going to show them and then show it to them. That's all there is to it. Don't tell them what to think about what they are going to see, just tell them what it is that they are going to see. Try it. You'll be amazed. Many designers do the opposite. They throw down a piece of work – something they might have sweated over for many weeks – and start talking about it as if their client had lived through the same voyage of discovery. Big mistake. And while you are babbling on, explaining what you've done, the poor client isn't listening. He or she is trying to assimilate something new and perhaps shocking. They are trying to evaluate what they are seeing. But by explaining what you are about to show, showing it, and then clamming up until asked a question, you can greatly assist the process.

Your presentation should also work when you are gone. The people you present to often have to present your proposal to other people, so providing a document summarizing your ideas is wise. But be careful how you brand this document. A client from a large company once told me, rather sourly, that she resented the way business consultants spread their logos across the documentation they presented to her. She found it tiresome and 'me, me, me,' she explained. I thought she had a point, and I've never done it. If I present a document to a client I always put their logo center stage. A client-first policy is rarely wrong, and applies to digital and projected presentations too.

Yet regardless of the psychological strategies, and the technical niceties of presenting, a presentation is always about personality. Your work has to be good, your thinking has to be faultless, your preparation has to be exhaustive. But you also have to strive to be liked. Talk clearly and good-humoredly about your work, maintain eye contact with everyone (especially the shy intern sitting in for experience), listen to questions when asked and conduct yourself like a decent human being.

Kim Hiorthøy

Kim Hiorthøy was born in 1973, in Trondheim, Norway. He is a musician and designer who also writes prose, makes films and draws. As a student, Hiorthøy studied fine art. He became enchanted by Andy Warhol, whom he encountered through the famous photographs of Nat Finkelstein, which led to his discovery of graphic design and the development of his cool, distinctive aesthetic. Hiorthøy is most famous in design circles for his sleek cover designs for the Norwegian experimental record label Rune Grammofon.

　　　　Hiorthøy cites a vast array of influences: Rudy VanderLans, Ellsworth Kelly, William Eggleston, Blue Note cover designer Reid Miles, the work of Designers Republic and early Mo'Wax sleeve designers Ben Drury and Will Bankhead. Hiorthøy has released a number of CDs of his music: wistful electronica and found audio detritus. He has produced a number of books, including the monograph *Tree Weekend*.

www.thisisrealart.com

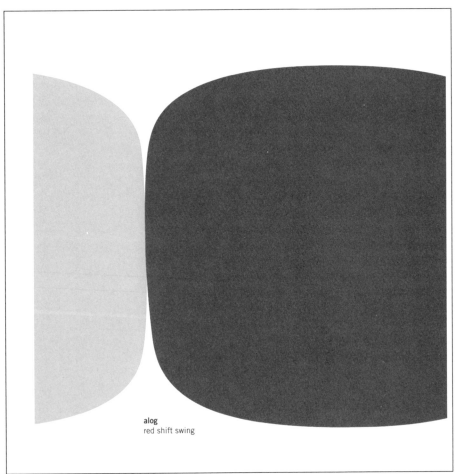

alog
red shift swing

Designed
by Kim Hiorthøy

AS When you look back on your design education are there elements to it that you didn't appreciate at the time but which now seem useful? KH I have no design education.

How have you learned about the business side of design? When I've visited schools I've sometimes felt that the business side is a bit overstressed. Or students have often asked me more about how much money I earn doing this or that job than about the work itself, which is fully understandable, but I think it's no use how good you are at pitching your ideas or how fancy your portfolio is if the actual work isn't good enough. Sometimes focusing too much on business can take a lot of joy out of work – and that means less quality. Learning by doing is always the best thing, and so you just learn by default when you start working.

Designers are often encouraged to specialize in one small area. Your design is stylistically diverse and you work in different media; what would you say to someone who wanted to do this? I often feel that it's a problem, this diversity. I envy people who do one thing and do that one thing really well because they've concentrated on it. I often feel like a jack-of-many-trades who doesn't master any of them. On the other hand, if anyone has the desire to work in different fields, or media, then they should do that. Diversity in knowledge is usually good no matter what you do. The more diverse your knowledge is, the more equipped you are. Follow your interests. If you are interested in many things, then go for them.

You work on your own. Do you ever think it would be nice to work in a studio surrounded by lots of people? Yes, I sometimes think that, but I don't know if I'd really be able to. I think I need to be alone in order not to be distracted, and in order to properly concentrate. In order to try stuff out it is sometimes necessary to do things you wouldn't necessarily be able to explain or argue for, and being alone frees me from that.

Where do your ideas come from? That is almost impossible to answer. Sometimes ideas come from seeing something someone else did. Sometimes they just come from trying something different than last time, or just thinking very hard about something (perhaps the job at hand), or not thinking at all and doing nothing. I don't know where ideas come from.

I know from working with you that you have integrity – you won't do something if it offends your sense of what is right. How sustainable is this in the modern world where money is everything and the penalties for failure are severe? Firstly, I think whether I have this integrity or not is very debatable. Secondly, I think it's as sustainable as you make it. In the end you decide what you want to do, and if the result of that is that you have to become a postman, in addition to trying to make it as a designer, then that is sustaining your integrity. Most people, given enough belief in themselves, are extremely resourceful and can do almost anything. If you are not happy with the premise under which you work, change the premise, or change what you do. Any integrity of any kind is lost anyway, the minute everyone simply decides integrity is not sustainable in 'the modern world'. The modern world is not some abstract force that rules our lives, it's just other people.

What would you say to an idealistic designer starting out today? Follow your interests; do what comes easy to you; do what gives you pleasure; and do it as much as you can. Don't wait for someone to ask you. If you keep at it and it feels right, eventually somebody will.

Do you have a design philosophy? Philosophy is: no philosophy!

Where do you stand on the 'Can design be art' debate? I don't care. The whole nature of art is precisely that it should try to defy its definition anyway. Design is a job. Whether the result becomes art or not, I couldn't give a rat's ass.

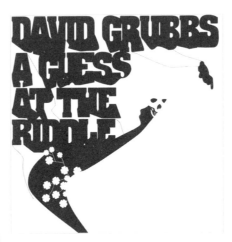

How to be a graphic designer, without losing your soul

Peter Stemmler

Peter Stemmler was born in 1966 in the former German Democratic Republic. After school and the army, Stemmler worked as a freelance press, wedding and portrait photographer, while studying social and political science at Humboldt University, Berlin. From 1992 to 1997 he studied communication design at the Kunsthochschule Weissensee, Berlin. After graduating, he worked as a designer-artist in Malaysia and Singapore, followed by a study exchange program at the London College of Printing, where he studied photography. In 1996, he completed internships at *Interview* magazine and Stefan Sagmeister's studio in New York, and worked as a designer and art director for Pandiscio Design, New York. Since 1999 he has been a freelance illustrator. He works for editorial and commercial clients including: *Playboy, Vanity Fair,* the *New Yorker, The New York Times,* ESPN, MTV, VH1, SCIFI Channel, Wieden & Kennedy and others. Since 1999, Stemmler has been a member of eboy and Quickhoney, his collaboration with Nana Rausch. They specialize in 'picture-based design solutions in all media.' They live with their one-year-old son in Brooklyn, New York.

www.quickhoney.com

Courtesy of Peter Stemmler

Designed by
by Peter Stemmler

AS How did you develop an interest in illustration? PS Accidentally. I was a photographer and did my diploma in graphic design. When I came to New York I got a job as a designer and had to do a brochure for BMW with really ugly photographic portraits. I just traced them in Illustrator and everybody really liked it, so I kept doing it as a hobby and went self-employed with it in 1999.

What role does the computer play in your work? It brings everything together: digital photography, illustration tools, communication and online gaming. I can work on up to three or four jobs at the same time from, and for, everywhere in the world. I cannot imagine going back to scanning, faxing and printing stuff out.

Do you manage to mix personal work with commercial work? Yes. If I want to try something new, I just do it, and make promo mailings out of it. Or I put it in those books where you send your stuff for free. Or I just put it up on the Quickhoney or eboy websites, and after a couple of months I get jobs with it. Oops, then it's not personal any more …

Do you worry about waking up one day and finding that your style is out of date? No. Right now I have four styles I work in, and maybe two I work on. Actually, I thought the simple vector stuff was already out of date, but hey, there will be a revival in like ten, fifteen years anyway, right?

What is your educational background? I apprenticed as a photographer for two years, spent two years studying sociology; five years studying communication design and went on to work three years as a designer. I've been a freelance illustrator/designer for five years and have been working as a photographer for twelve.

When you look back, what strikes you as good about your education? I had a lot of time to find out what I wanted to do. Up until the age of thirty, I was traveling a lot while I was studying (exchange programs and work in England, Malaysia, the US). Then I picked the place (Brooklyn, New York) where I wanted to live and work.

How did you learn about the business side of being an illustrator? Since I was a photographer for a while already, and working as a designer, it was no big deal. But my internship at *Interview* magazine was really helpful. And if you collaborate with other people, like I do, you have a lot more chances to learn stuff from each other.

How do you attract new clients, and is your business profitable? I do a mailing with new stuff, maybe two times a year. But most of my work I get from people I've worked with for years. These people often switch magazines or companies and take me with them, and yes, my business is profitable.

If you were starting your career over again what would you do differently? I don't know. I don't think I did anything really wrong. Maybe I'd get a good office chair right away. My advice is: don't save on the monitor – get a good one; go to work on a bicycle; do some kind of sport like running; don't work every weekend; drink your coffee with sugar then you don't have to eat all those candy bars; get a cell phone. If you start becoming good in certain online games, you are playing too much. And don't write business e-mails when you are drunk, do it the next morning!

What do you say to young designers starting out today? Ha, most important – don't work alone. Don't compromise if the client doesn't pay accordingly. Have fun or look for something else to do like cooking, architecture, pro online gaming, writing or music.

Designed by
by Peter Stemmler

Chapter 8 / p.119 – 129
Self-promotion *'I don't want to be famous, I just want my peers to like what I do'*
Cultivating a reputation – Work done for the portfolio, not the bank balance – Design
competitions – Professional organizations – Attending lectures and events – Maintaining
relationships with art colleges – Dealing with the press.

The big design groups aside, design studios and individual designers promote themselves in a notoriously haphazard way. It's different with the big multinational design groups. They are pumped full of marketing steroids, and they know how to get a foot in the doors of big rich corporations hungry to spend millions having their brand image burnished. The big groups have the money and the expertise to promote themselves by using sophisticated marketing and communication techniques. But since many of them no longer even call themselves 'designers' – preferring the term 'brand consultants' – there is probably not much for the independent-minded designer to learn from them. Nevertheless, smaller design groups and individual designers have to promote themselves, too. We've already discussed the benefits of word of mouth exposure in generating new work for studios, but in truth, what we are talking about is the cultivation of a reputation. Designers depend almost entirely on their reputations for their livelihoods. It pays to have a good one.

Acquiring a reputation isn't easy; you have to earn it and it has to be forged out of the raw materials of your personality and your work. But there's a problem here: notions of fame and celebrity have invaded design's body politic. The design world's obsession with celebrity hasn't reached the feeding frenzy proportions of the music industry or Hollywood, but graphic design now has its own star system: a celebrity A-list of big name designers, followed by a B-list and C-list of less well-known individuals, and, for all we know, if we scour magazines and websites around the world, we might find a Z-list, too.

The upshot of all this is that the design world has come to confuse fame and celebrity with reputation. It is now possible, even as a moderately successful designer, to be written about, to be interviewed in magazines and to be invited to lecture at colleges and speak at design conferences. This used to be done by the great and the good of the design world: designers who had acquired eminence over decades. Today, such is the appetite for graphic design, many designers – and not just the establishment figures – have the spotlight thrown upon them. We've also witnessed studios arriving on the scene boasting some sparky work and attracting instant attention. Magazines write about them, and despite having been in existence for less time than it takes to blow your nose, they manage to publish a monograph. Suddenly, the studio acquires minor celebrity status. Other young designers look admiringly at this and think: it must be good to be the object of so much adoration.

Not much wrong with that, you might think: but in fact, unwarranted attention can be destructive. Being the 'next big thing' is rarely desirable. It will perhaps help propel the studio forward for a few months, by opening a few doors and attracting a few new clients. It will certainly be fleetingly enjoyable to have your views sought by design journalists, and to have your work featured in magazines and sexy new design books. But unless this interest is built on real foundations, it will evaporate. Just flip back through the design press from the past three or four years, and you'll see what I mean: you'll find designers tipped for success that no-one's heard of since, you'll find reviews of monographs from studios that don't exist any more.

There is even a theory, currently gaining widespread credence in design circles, that predicts that if you have too much fame it boils over and scalds your feet. Immediately after his epochal one-man show at London's Victoria & Albert Museum in 1988, and the publication of a best-selling monograph,[1] the British designer Neville Brody went bankrupt, and for the next decade was forced to find work abroad. More recently, in a reader's poll run by the British journal *Creative Review,* the eminent British designer Peter Saville failed to retain his crown as the 'Best Graphic Designer Working Today', a category he'd won on two previous occasions. This was unexpected: the designer had just enjoyed a year of staggering success. He'd held a much-admired one-man show at London's Design Museum; he'd published a long-awaited monograph,[2] and he'd enjoyed an unprecedented (for a designer) amount of coverage from the non-design press. In an article *Creative Review's* editor, Patrick Burgoyne, reflected on this: 'Peter Saville in particular seems to have suffered from the exposure afforded by last year's Design Museum exhibition and book: from winning best graphic designer two years in a row he now fails to make the top three. It's no reflection on his work or his long term place in the design firmament, I'm sure, but perhaps an example of the contrary nature of whatever passes for fame in the graphics micro-world'.[3]

'Micro-world' is right. Fame in graphic design circles is a bit like fame in dentistry; it doesn't travel far. If you are a member of a boy band, your views and opinions will be eagerly sought by print and electronic media. But no-one is interested in the thoughts of graphic designers beyond the confines of graphic design, and in truth, very few graphic designers are able to rise to the occasion. When exposed and cross-examined outside of the cozy world of design, graphic designers tend to come over as self-centered and only interested in graphic design.

The lesson is simple: we must not confuse admiration and respect with fame or celebrity. A number of groups have sought to acquire fame and celebrity by hyping themselves and behaving more like boy bands than design groups. In recent years there have been some spectacular culprits. The ostentatious gesture of the bravura book project is a typical ruse: a big fat book arrives on the scene, stuffed with visual pyrotechnics, which on the surface appears to show the group as dynamic and boundary-stretching, but on closer inspection is revealed to be egotistical and pointless graphic doodling. And for those who play this game, it is dangerously easy to believe your own hype. It usually ends up with some sort of implosion or dramatic reversal of fortunes.

[1] In 1988 Brody published the first of his two monographs, which became best-selling graphic design books – combined sales now exceed 120,000 copies. The accompanying exhibition at the V&A attracted over 40,000 visitors before touring Europe and Japan.

[2] The book was called *Designed by Peter Saville* (edited by Emily King). The exhibition was called 'The Peter Saville Show', Design Museum, London, 2003.

[3] *Creative Review,* October 2004. The designer Mark Farrow won, with Michael C Place and Stefan Sagmeister as runners-up.

Getting noticed

Yet, if fame and celebrity are illusory, and no guarantee of success or lasting recognition, you still need to get noticed. You can't hide in a hole in the ground and expect to be spotted by clients. There are various legitimate actions you can take in order to get noticed. In the next few pages we'll explore some of these options. However, nothing works as well as the simple expedient of doing great work. If you do great work, if you do effective, original and striking work full of emotional or intellectual resonance, you are unlikely to go unnoticed.

This willingness to recognize and acknowledge good work done by others is one of the design world's more endearing features. And it's just as well, because this is how reputations are forged. A reputation begins in the design world, and only when it is firmly rooted there does it spread out into the bigger world of clients, commerce and the culture beyond. Designers with good reputations in the design world slowly begin to acquire a reputation elsewhere. If you are one of the big muscular design groups I talked about earlier, then you can work at building a reputation in the world of business – but for small independent designers, this is out of the question. You have to start within the design world, confident that if your reputation is strong it will be picked up by alert clients, and you will find yourself worming out of the sealed-off world of design into the bigger world of clients, money and connections and opportunities.

Besides doing great work, there are one or two other things you can do to help the process: you can be generous about the work of other designers; you can help new designers through teaching, mentoring and offering work experience; you can give talks and take part in conferences; you can write about design (and not about yourself); and you can conduct yourself ethically.

Work done for the portfolio, not the bank balance

Designers often imagine that if they write their own briefs they will produce the sort of work that will boost their profile. This sometimes works. Self-initiated projects are often necessary for the individual's – or studio's – psychic health, and the urge to experiment and explore is perfectly reasonable. But the blunt truth is that clients are simply not as impressed with self-initiated projects as they are with a great piece of work done in response to a real live brief. By all means, do personal work, but do it for personal reasons, and don't kid yourself that it will open doors.

Instead, try and find a client who you can do a deal with. Try and find a client who will let you do some boundary-defying work in exchange for a substantially reduced fee. This might be work undertaken for a good cause: a charity or a non-profit organization. Or it could be an opportunity to give your skills to a client who, in the normal course of events, might find you too expensive. There is an unwritten rule that states the more money a client spends the less freedom they permit, but if you can find one – a real living and breathing client – who will permit and encourage you to produce ground-breaking work, it will be much more beneficial to your reputation than a self-initiated project.

But this must not be used as an opportunity for indulgence. Quite the opposite: it is not about pleasing yourself. Despite the ostensible freedom that you have negotiated, and despite the absence of fees, you must be resolved to work with all the gusto, imagination and focus, you would muster for a job with fifty times the budget. Because in graphic design circles, what really gets a client's red blood cells circulating is seeing work that *works* – aesthetically and commercially.

Where do you find such a client? Start by approaching a subject, or an area, that is normally devoid of good design: don't approach a cool sports brand or a publisher who only produces beautifully crafted books. Go and see a local garden center or a dentist. Or you can do what we did at Intro and design CD covers for reggae and dub labels. Here's what happened: an old and valued friend of mine came to see me and said he was putting together a CD label called Blood and Fire to release Jamaican dub and reggae classics from the seventies. Although my friend had backing from some prominent figures in the UK music industry, he didn't have an open checkbook and budgets were tight. I recognized an opportunity to do some great work. Original Jamaican record sleeves have a visceral, untutored kick greatly appreciated by fans of the music. But the repackaging of Jamaican music by American and European labels tended to be patronizing and clichéd; it was all palm tress and Rasta colors. Here was an area of music packaging that hadn't been touched by design. I told my friend that if he trusted us to go down a previously untried path we would create something remarkable for him.

Mat Cook took on the task of designing the first batch of Blood and Fire covers. At this time, graphic design was in thrall to the newly arrived Apple Macintosh computers: there was a template-like, digital-sameness to most of the graphic design that was around at the time. With typical contrariness, Mat headed off in the opposite direction. He got out a hammer, some rusty nails, some old fencing and a few cans of industrial paint, and he made a series of crumbly installations that looked as if Robert Rauschenberg had been working in a scrap-yard in Kingston, Jamaica. When Mat's sculpture-like installations appeared on CD covers, not only were the covers praised, but hard-nosed music retailers and distributors admitted that the covers were a significant factor in the label's early success.[4]

At a crucial time in the history of Intro, this brought us a welcome injection of attention. All sorts of people including non-music-industry clients approached us with offers of work as a result. Journalists called asking to do profiles, and students wrote asking for jobs – the two sure-fire signs that told us we were on the map. Yet, looked at in strict accounting terms, doing this work was a short-term disaster. We took a loss on all the work we did for the label. But this was carefully monitored: we evaluated the sacrifice needed, and we had faith in Mat's ability to create genuinely iconoclastic work. We made sure we didn't let our outside costs get out of control (fencing and rusty nails are cheap), but we were unstinting in the amount of time we gave to the project.

King Tubby, *Dub Gone Crazy,*
Yabby U, *King Tubby's Prophesy of Dub*
Album covers by Mat Cook at Intro

4   Mat didn't even like dub. But as the great Blue Note designer Reid Miles proved, you don't have to like the music to do great covers for it. Miles famously didn't like jazz, and never listened to the music of the artists he had to create cover designs for. As these two examples prove, if you have sufficient cultural awareness you can produce work that is culturally appropriate.

It paid off: over subsequent years, this work generated a vast amount of new work from firms, bands and other record labels who were admirers of the Blood and Fire look, and it enhanced our reputation at a critical moment of our development. Every designer and studio should have a client like Blood and Fire.

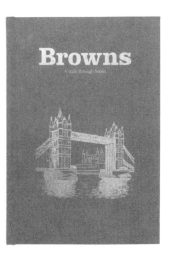

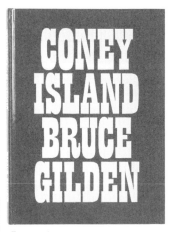

Browns A walk through books
and *Coney Island Bruce Gilden*
designed by Browns

The design group Browns, founded by designer Jonathan Ellery, chose a different path. Since their inception Browns have published their own books. Subject matter is invariably image-based, and their published output to date adds up to a substantial achievement and has contributed significantly to building Browns' reputation as one of the UK's most accomplished and craft-based design studios. But Ellery didn't set out to produce books that would act as promo-trailers for his company. 'On reflection, our early book projects were in response to what we felt at the time to be a very corporate, clinical, graphic design world', he notes. 'The incentive and the energy to produce our own books came from a mixture of desperation, no clients and a love of the printed page. I wish I could say there was a commercial or PR strategy in place, but there wasn't. At the time, our accountant told us that it was pointless and to this day still struggles with the concept.'

Their accountant should wise up. The strategy has paid off handsomely. Today, Browns work for a diverse range of clients and while their success is down to more than the books they produce, their small catalog of lovingly crafted publications appears to have made a substantial contribution to the studio's growth and reputation. As Ellery explains: 'People have always found our books of interest, which is very gratifying. They seem to find their way into design, photography and art magazines which has given us profile over the years, and in a way has defined us as a studio. We do a lot of other things, but the books seem to be the projects with the most resonance. It continually surprises me when I get a call from the likes of fashion designer Dries Van Noten asking us to design a book for him. Over the years he had acquired some of our publishing projects and related to them.'

Ellery's reluctance to formalize Browns' publishing activities into a calculated promotional activity paradoxically makes them all the more effective as promotional tools. The books are done from conviction – from love, you might say – which makes their impact all the more potent. 'We're now enjoying a time', he notes, 'where the books we have designed and published are strangely creating business opportunities. Image library Photonica is another example of a client paying good money for us to design a book for them. In a funny sort of way our publishing activities – a purely cultural gesture on our part – has made good business sense.'

Design competitions

Opinion is split on design competitions. For many designers, the notion of 'competing' like athletes in a race is anathema. And you can see their point: winning a design award, detractors will note, doesn't necessarily mean that you are 'the best'. For a start, if you don't enter, you can't win. On top of this, you usually have to pay to enter so only those who can afford the entry fees can take part, which means that if you win a design award you are in fact only winning 'The Best of What's Been Entered' award. Furthermore, you also have to submit your work to the scrutiny of fellow designers who are, typically, your rivals in business. How can you be sure of their impartiality?

Other designers take a more trusting view: they make a point of entering every competition possible on the reasonable premise that if they win they are gifted an invaluable promotional opportunity, and receive that most precious of designer accolades: peer approval. (Winners also acquire drab-looking 'statuettes' or faux parchment scrolls decorated with bad calligraphy to display in their studios. Which prompts the question: why do design awards usually look so dreadful?)

And despite all the moaning and controversy that surrounds the winning entries ('Why did they choose that? I did something identical six years ago') it usually is the good stuff that wins. Something else I've noticed: I've sat on quite a few design juries, and I'm always impressed by how generous designers are about each other's work. Sure, you meet some sour and resentful individuals, but they are the exception rather than the norm. The first time I sat on a jury I expected it to be a snakepit of fear and loathing, but my fellow jurors were generous, considerate and tirelessly fair. And this has been true of the other juries I've sat on (not that this precludes some absurd decisions from time to time).

All scruples about design competitions, their artificiality, their fundamental unfairness, vanish when we win. It is very sweet to win a design prize, and winners must publicize and exploit their successes. Send a short e-mail to your clients announcing your win (don't crow about it – mention a few other winners, too) and never forget to include your client in any celebrations – you wouldn't have won it without them.

Professional organizations

There are numerous professional bodies offering support, advice and education for the fledgling designer.5 Most countries have them; a list of established bodies and institutions appears at the end of this book. Most require membership fees and in return you get helpful advice and useful opportunities to learn more about design and design-related matters from fellow professionals. Of course, some designers prefer to remain aloof from communal activities: they see joining design institutions as a step towards losing their independent status and becoming linked to the design establishment; they tend to dismiss professional organizations as smug and self-admiring. Others, with more clubbable instincts, relish the camaraderie that comes with banding together with like-minded individuals, and become energetic participants.

In describing itself the AIGA sets out its aims and intentions: 'AIGA sets the national agenda for the role of design in its economic, social, political, cultural and creative contexts.
5   AIGA is the oldest and largest membership association for professionals engaged in the discipline, practice and culture of designing. Founded as the American Institute of Graphic Arts in 1914 as a small, exclusive club. AIGA now represents more than 16,000 designers through national activities and local programs developed by 48 chapters and more than 150 student groups.' www.aiga.org

The fundamental altruism of the various professional bodies and associations, and the degree to which they promote the interests of design and designers, cannot be questioned. In recent years, they have made conspicuous and vigorous efforts to become more inclusive, with particular emphasis on helping and encouraging students and recent graduates. They run lectures, educational sessions and have made extensive and effective use of online material. But, inevitably, in their attempt to become all-encompassing, they tend to represent the mainstream: if your interests are in the margins and slipstreams of design and contemporary culture, they are perhaps less relevant to you. Whether you join is a matter of personal judgment.

Attending conferences and lectures

There is today no shortage of design conferences for the design enthusiast to attend. They are held all over the world in attractive cities that no-one minds very much having to visit. They are organized by the design press, by publishers, by professional bodies and by arts centers, and provide congenial opportunities to hear other points of view and to discuss pressing issues with fellow designers. But are design conferences – usually held in the sorts of hotels and conference centers that make living in a tent on the edge of a busy road seem attractive – any good? Do they offer anything substantial to the young designer? They are certainly not cheap to attend, yet large numbers of people flock to hear famous designers talk and show off their work. They can't be that bad.

6 *Eye* 49,
Autumn 2003.

The writer and conference organizer Alice Twemlow, wrote an article in *Eye* magazine about the design conference phenomenon: 'Design conferences are the places where we hear designers' voices most literally,' she wrote. 'Yet, of all the apparatus and artifacts that the graphic design community uses as professional buoys, conferences are the least evolved and most perplexing. Books, annuals, magazines and exhibitions are, after all, native territory to graphic designers, and academic curricula and professional associations are firmly established in the discipline's psyche. Conferences, however, are relatively new additions to the field and they sit somewhat uneasily within it. Their styrofoam coffee cups, skirted buffet tables, 'Hello my name is …' badges and PowerPoint presentations bring with them the foreign whiff of Shriners' conventions and the annual industry gatherings of travel agents, car insurance brokers or dentists.'

Twemlow is spot on with her 'styrofoam coffee cups' and 'skirted buffet tables'; and her comments about the sometimes uneasy fit between designers and the conference arena are shrewd. But having attended conferences both as a participant and as a visitor, I've always learned something – even if it's only to be thoroughly prepared if you're a speaker, and to take some Tylenol along if you're planning any late-night socializing.

Not as grandiose as conferences, lectures are an essential part of the education of a designer – especially if the lecturer is a good speaker with an interesting tale to tell. Show and tell sessions can provide invaluable insight into the creative process. I've often been forced to re-evaluate a designer's work after attending his or her lecture. There's something about the elemental format of the lecture room that enables us to get to the heart of the matter. In design, we too often assume that there is only ever one way to do things, but listening to designers, especially those from different cultures, alerts us to other possibilities. I took part in a lecture session with some Japanese designers in Tokyo. Their work was exciting, but they were excessively modest about it – almost apologetic. And while I'd never advocate arrogance, they made me realize that you can be too humble.

Maintaining relationships with art colleges

There are many good reasons why it's worth maintaining connections with your former college, or forging links with new ones. Designers have an unwritten duty to pass on their experience and give support to the next generation of designers. It is relatively easy to do this. Colleges are keen to have visits and lectures from professionals. And since the colleges and schools usually pay for our time, there is no excuse for not doing it. Many designers develop a taste for teaching and discover an aptitude for mentoring. Some become external examiners, while others enjoy giving occasional talks and presentations. But maintaining links with schools and colleges needn't be just about altruism. Designers have much to gain in practical terms from associations with educational establishments.

In an interview I conducted with Paula Scher of Pentagram for *Design Week*, she identified one of the fringe benefits of teaching: '… It's very good for recruiting. I get to hire the best students,' she stated, before going on to say, '… teaching is a great way to have the sort of dialogue I can't have with my clients: about aesthetics, about color theory, about design theory. It's very beneficial to have this other perspective.'

So, teaching is good for the soul, and good for recruiting. And, I'd add another benefit: today's students are, in some cases, tomorrow's clients. I was once contacted by a woman who ran a large government department dealing with education matters. She was looking for a design company to undertake a large-scale project. She said that normally this would be handled in-house by her team of designers. They rarely, she explained, commissioned external independent studios. But on this occasion, the project was too big for her team, and in order to find a suitable design company she had asked one of her designers to recommend a studio. By chance, the designer she consulted had attended a talk I had given at his college. He'd been impressed and put forward my name. The woman visited our studio, and after the inevitable pitch the project was won.

Now, this is not going to happen every time you give a talk or show some work at an art school. The point here is that it *can* happen, and therefore you should view contact with colleges both as an opportunity to give something to the next generation, and also with the confidence that your altruism might be repaid at some time in the future.

Dealing with the design press

Designers imagine that coverage in the design press – an in-depth profile, or a casual mention – means instant success: they envision clients rushing to hire them after reading about them and seeing their work in the glossy pages of one of the sleek design zines. Alas, it is rarely like this.

Exposure in the design press is an important step on the way to acquiring a reputation in the design world, but it should not be mistaken for a passport to instant success. Exposure in the design press is desirable and worthwhile, but its effects are cumulative. People need to see two or three pieces of work, or read a few articles or news items, before the word of mouth process starts in earnest. And of course, when we get our opportunities to bask in the spotlight, we have to be sure that we get everything right and don't use the moment to make fools of ourselves.

How do you get your work into the design press? Editors and journalists are constantly on the look-out for fresh voices and new faces. It's their job, and if you are any good they will find you. But there are ways to help them find you. Develop the habit of sending magazines details of your latest work. Include a brief description of the project in question, the name of the client and any other relevant information. Keep it brief: if an editor is interested someone will contact you about the details. The document, with accompanying visuals, must be sent before the subject is due to be exposed to the public, or its intended audience, and it should be sent in plenty of time for the magazine's deadline. Most magazines want striking work, they want newness, and they want high-quality images.

You need to study the design press and decide which magazines and periodicals (online and print) your work is most suited to. It can sometimes be beneficial to appear in a less obvious magazine from time to time, although it can be hard to persuade editors who don't regularly feature graphic design to report graphic design stories. You also need to decide which sections in magazines would suit your project. A call to the magazine will enable you to find out the publication's deadlines, its policy on receiving submissions and who to send your work to. Look out for special features such as regional surveys or analysis of specialist sectors such as digital design or moving image. Timing is vital: miss an issue and you'll have to wait another month before your work can be included, by which time the project might be old news.

You must also keep in mind questions of confidentiality (does your client want their product exposed before it is launched?). Most clients enjoy seeing the work they commissioned written about in a magazine, but it is essential to always get their permission. However, the most important thing to remember is that journalists are inundated with material, and although most of what they receive is dire, there is no shortage of good projects for them to feature. Consequently, they will only use a tiny percentage of what they are sent, so only send your best work. And I've always made a point of not sending material to more than one publication at a time. All magazines demand exclusives, so you will quickly run out of friends if you are seen to be flogging your wares to everyone. Choose which magazine is best suited to your project, and send your information to them, and them alone.

Once you are known as a reliable supplier of exciting visual material, journalists will contact you to see what projects you have in hand, but until that day comes you need to get in touch with them. Journalists might also discover that you are a reliable supplier of quotes, and invite you to contribute comments to articles: this way you get to spout off on your favorite topics.

If you are really hot stuff, you might be made the subject of a profile. Unless you are very confident, I'd avoid giving interviews over the telephone. Journalists are fallible, and sometimes comments and observations are reported wrongly, with dire consequences. One of the first magazine interviews I did was conducted by telephone. The result was a disaster. A busy journalist spoke to me about some work I'd done: I could sense his haste. In his rush he confused my client with a rival company, and I spent weeks patching up the rift that opened up between my upset client and myself. Try and do interviews via e-mail. This gives you time to think about your answers and avoid gaffs. Some journalists prefer to do interviews face-to-face, and you have no choice in the matter: but take it slowly, and don't be shy about supplementing your answers via e-mail after the interview.

Another possibility is to offer to write articles for the design press. Editors often welcome contributions from working designers. You have to be able to write, of course. Although a good copy editor can knock rough-edged prose into shape, editors usually prefer to commission someone whose prose doesn't need too much surgery. But if you have an insight into some aspect of design, suggest it to an editor.

Designers need regular injections of exposure, but don't let it become a fixation. The benefits are fleeting and transitory at best. Think about acquiring a lasting reputation for good work done consistently over a number of years – and not over the past month. If you want to be famous, the first thing you have to do is stop wanting to be famous.

Corey Holms

Corey Holms was born in 1970 and graduated from the California Institute of the Arts (CalArts) in 1996. Until recently he was an art director at Crew in Los Angeles, where he worked on posters, ad campaigns and print media to support major motion pictures. His clients included Warner Brothers, Universal, Imagine, Paramount, 20th Century Fox, Sony and HBO. Before Concept Arts, he worked for Sapient Corporation on websites for a range of corporate clients. From 1996 to 1999 he worked at Frankfurt Balkind, where he designed the logo for the *Sopranos* television series, as well as poster designs for the Getty Museum. Since 1996, as well as holding down full-time employment, he has maintained a thriving freelance practice doing work for numerous clients in the fashion and architecture sectors. He currently resides in Brea, California, with his wife and twin daughters.

www.coreyholms.com

Designed
by Corey Holms

What inspired you to become a graphic designer? CH Record sleeves and comic books. I didn't have an art class in school after the fourth grade, including the first two years of college. But I was obsessive about collecting things that were designed. Then I started noticing that a lot of the things I was buying were done by the same people: The Designers Republic, Dave McKean, Bill Sienkiewicz, Neville Brody, Malcolm Garrett and many more.

After two years of college, I decided to try my hand at art. I drove out to CalArts to talk to someone about it and happened to meet Jeff Keedy, the then director of the design program at the school. I was interested in doing some form of fine arts that involved typography. Keedy said that design was the only program that allowed students to take type classes. So I decided to be a designer at that point. I think I would have failed miserably as a fine artist, and it was rather fortuitous that design found me.

Do you look back on aspects of your education that didn't seem important at the time, but which now appear important? Many: I wish I had paid more attention in my classes overall, but specifically to my type design class (taught to us through calligraphy, which I thought was a waste of time), and design history, where I slept through several of the classes. I think that it is incredibly important to understand the history of design, otherwise you make glaring errors in your choice of typefaces. I have seen so many designers choose inaccurate or inappropriate typefaces for projects because they have no knowledge of what the connotations are. At one company I worked, a designer consistently chose 1930s typefaces for horror movies. For every horror presentation, there would be a selection of posters that looked like they were designed for the Orient Express, and the designer never understood why the typefaces were wrong.

You worked for a big design company, and yet managed to do personal projects. Can you talk about this? When you work for a big design company, there are often fewer chances for personal vision than if you work in a small shop. The personal projects are a way for me to see a project from inception to hand-off all on my own. It keeps me honest, if you know what I mean. It would be very easy to lose some skills that aren't used in the day job (like typesetting), and I do it partially for the experience.

I also do it because I love design. I can't stop doing design (much to the chagrin of my wife). I stay up late at nights on the sofa with a bad movie playing, while I work on a typeface, or on a self-initiated project. I find that a day job doesn't afford me the opportunities to do everything I want (like type design, or experimentation with forms), so I do it on my own time after everyone has gone to sleep.

What are the advantages of working for big studios? For me, it's primarily security. Although the advice I get from all of my design friends is to set up my own studio, I have a family to take care of and the thought of the price of major surgery, or missing a mortgage payment absolutely terrifies me. It's the main reason I stayed at a large agency. I got a regular salary, paid vacation and health insurance (among other benefits). I could never take a vacation if I worked for myself, and my nerves would be a mess.

I am a very bad businessman, so I need someone to take care of that aspect of the job for me. To run your own studio you need to be a great designer, an account executive and an accountant. I struggle enough with being a designer; I can't do the other two. Another advantage in working for a large agency is the clientele. I'd never have got to work for so many wonderful clients if it had not been for the safety and the peace of mind they get from the corporate machine.

You worked for an astonishing array of clients. Were you able to pick and choose the jobs that came in? Unless there is a real issue with either the project or the client, I work on what is assigned to me. There have been occasions where a client is not appreciative of the work I do, so it was decided to take me off that account and for me to concentrate on another account where the client likes what I do. But beyond that, it's pretty much whatever is in the shop at the moment.

Since I am not financially independent, the day job has afforded me the opportunity to choose projects that are the most rewarding to me, in my private practice. Of course there are sacrifices that must be made – the private practice gets nowhere close to the amount of time it deserves, but that's a concession I regrettably have to make. Hopefully, in the future the two schedules will reach a state of equilibrium, but for now that's not an attainable goal.

How do you approach jobs that on the surface appear to offer little scope for creative input? Sometimes those are the most interesting. I know that sounds like a rehearsed answer, but it's true. When given complete free rein, I tend to run around in circles for quite a while before settling into the ideas I wish to pursue. But with limited creative scope, you can sometimes really get into the details. I'll try to set little goals for myself like custom-kerning an entire document, so that at the very least the type will be perfect.

Recently I designed a brochure that needed to have a French WWII feel to it (but was very restrictive design-wise), so I researched the type of the period and made certain to use only historically accurate typefaces and typographic details. It was incredible fun, and I learned some lessons that I can't wait to use on an appropriate personal project. I think the key lies in finding one special thing about the project and getting lost in that particular bit of minutiae. I'm not saying that every single job is like that, but you can find something in the majority of them.

What do you think about the current design scene? I am amazed by how quickly design cannibalizes itself. Since we live in a global culture, trends and influences spread much quicker than they used to. The current design scene assimilates 'new' within a matter of weeks, and spits it out on a commercial level six months later. I don't know if this is a good or a bad thing. But I'm interested in seeing how this affects design ten years from now. Just in the period since the internet has come to prominence, there has been a profound change in the way designers work, communicate and source inspiration.

There are designers who currently make their living designing things for other designers to consume. I cannot think of another service industry that has its own sub-industry catering to itself. There aren't chefs that only cook for other chefs – and before you say it's because that's a non-creative industry, what about architecture? I can't think of any architects who design only for other architects. But designers do.

Who inspires you? Wim Crouwel, Peter Saville, Michael Place, Otl Aicher and lots of random little things I'll see through the day. I carry a camera with me everywhere I go, and I'm always taking pictures. There are times when I see a color combination that I know I won't be able to remember, so the camera is handy for all sorts of cataloguing. I find things all the time that are inspirational. I've recently started a series of posters that are based on jpegs that I saved to my hard drive, but somehow have become corrupted. They're beautiful shifted color grids that have inspired me to figure out the pattern and try to replicate it in Illustrator. I guess everyday stuff inspires me as well.

I found a discarded paper lying in the gutter the other day. Other bits of trash were laid over the top of it, cropping it in the most interesting way. It was completely eye-catching. It pissed off everyone I was with, but I got my camera out and stepped into the street to get the angle I wanted.

What do you say to a young designer starting out today? Pay attention. Honestly, I think that's the best advice I was ever given. Just stop talking, and start watching and listening. I was very arrogant coming out of school, and missed out on a lot of great opportunities because of it. I could have accomplished so much more if I wasn't so concerned about trying to convince people that I was always right and had the best solution (and a good chunk of the time, you'll find that you aren't correct). I'm not saying you should let go of your ideas, I'm just saying you should listen to the comments that others are making.

Where does the creative process begin? You could argue that the creative process begins with the decision to become a designer. From that moment on, everything you see and do feeds your visual intelligence, and contributes to the making of a designer. It's one of the best things about being a designer: seeing design everywhere, and taking inspiration from anything. You can't turn off the fact that you're a designer: you will always be tuned in and receiving. Or at least you should be.

When we look at good design – the stuff that inspires us – we want to emulate it. Infuriatingly, the best design always looks effortless. We are convinced we can do it too. But when it comes to it, we find it is much more difficult than we at first thought. So what are the skills you need to do good work? I've already mentioned talent, and I've stressed that the discipline of graphic design, as it is practised today, allows a wide and generous interpretation of the word. Graphic design is a bit like the game of rugby. At school I was forced to play this semi-barbaric, often violent ball game, in mud and freezing rain. My school's Rottweiler-like gym teacher was a rugby fanatic. After picking the best players he'd glare at the unsporty residue – the ones who hadn't been picked for his team – and say gloatingly: 'Don't worry, there's a place for all types in rugby. Big or small, fat or thin, there's a role for everyone.' There isn't much physical violence in graphic design, but there is room for nearly everyone with any sort of talent.

Let's assume that talent is a given. What else do you need? Industriousness, dedication and a love of your craft are indispensable. Obvious really, but if you can't say that you have all three of these qualities, then you should perhaps consider another career. I'd say that it is also essential to have a questioning attitude to your work. If you don't question everything that is put in front of you, then you run the risk of being compliant and submissive, and these two qualities are not conducive to producing great work; they are the qualities of mediocrity. By urging you to adopt a questioning attitude, I'm not advocating a carping or complaining approach. I'm saying that you should be sceptical (but not bitter) towards the business of design. Finally, you need to acquire a 'voice'. I was tempted to say 'style' here, but voice is more accurate, because it is more personal and it suggests humanistic qualities. How do you acquire a voice? This is not easily answered. A design voice, a tone, is forged by three main elements.

In an interview, Saul Bass noted a problem encountered by young designers and students: 'They are not privy to process,' he noted. 'They may have the illusion that these things really spring full-blown out of the head of some designer. This is a very unsettling perception for young people, because they struggle with their work. They have a go at it ... They redo ... It gets better ... It slips ... It gets worse ... it comes back ... It comes together. And maybe it's something that's pretty good, even excellent. But they say to themselves, "Gee, it comes hard and it's so difficult. Am I really suited for this?"' Reproduced in *Essays on Design 1: AGI's Designers of Influence*, 1997.

It is firstly a question of creative conviction: you need to have a vision – a clear and informed understanding – of what is good, and what has real worth. It should not be a rigid creed, but it needs to be strong enough to stop you being blown about helplessly. It can be either a 'philosophical' creed ('I think design is about improving social conditions') or it can be an aesthetic creed ('I only use sans serif fonts'). It can even be a combination of both, but you have to believe in something. Secondly, it is a question of personality: you need to have an inner confidence that allows you to trust your creative instincts – although there is always room for doubt and self-scrutiny. And thirdly, it is a question of an awareness of fashion, cultural trends and history. As designers we often like to think we are above fashion, but we rarely are. The human appetite for novelty, and the tidal pull of the zeitgeist, makes staying aloof from fashion almost impossible for most designers. Traditional graphic design thinking warns designers of the perils of fashion, and certainly if you are a slave to fashion, you will become its victim. Yet all good designers are attuned to fashion: they cherry-pick from new and emergent trends; they adopt certain stylistic gestures and avoid other over-exposed modes of expression that once seemed new and fresh. But they are careful and selective in what they take. And the way to keep the pull of fashion in check is to know your design history – which, thanks to design's protean nature, means 'yesterday' as well as a hundred years ago.

Before we look at the practical factors that have to be contended with during the creative process, it's worth mentioning a fixation, held by many designers, that has a great influence on the way designers function in the post-modern world where everything, seemingly, has already been done. I'm talking about the concept of originality. Most designers are untroubled by the notion of originality, but others are obsessed with it, and I see many problems caused by the delusional quest for originality. In my view originality is an overrated and misunderstood quality in contemporary graphic design. Copying is bad, no question. Infringing someone's copyright (stealing their work or their ideas) for personal gain is immoral, not to mention illegal in most countries. But the only people who copy are the terminally second-rate and the downright dishonest, whereas the good designer freely borrows and adapts from sources in precisely the way artists have done for centuries. And furthermore, the good designer readily admits to this 'appropriation'. It is a quality of many good designers that their influences and sources are clearly visible and readily acknowledged.

Let's not kid ourselves that day-of-creation originality is possible in graphic design. Designers are locked in an interconnecting matrix of tradition and shared sensibility. All designers can hope to do is acquire a voice, a fingerprint, that they can call their own. This voice, paradoxically, is most readily acquired by opening ourselves up to the influence of other schools of design and visual art. My personal philosophy is that it is right to borrow and to be influenced by visual material as long as you are not slavishly copying it, and as long as you use these sources to make something demonstrably new. Yet many good designers find this hard. They have grown up in a culture where originality is prized, and as a consequence they take refuge in bland, non-expressive modes of design for fear of being called 'unoriginal'. The British designer Julian House, who I worked with closely at Intro for a number of years, has clear views on this question. 'I don't believe in originality as an absolute,' he states. 'I think it's more to do with interesting twists on existing forms. Borrowing from the Modernist designers of the recent past, for instance, is not plagiarism; it's more a continuation of the processes and ideas that they set in motion. I'm influenced by Polish poster art of the 1960s, which was influenced by Pop Art and Surrealism, and which in turn appropriated commercial art, comic book art, cinema and Victorian engravings, etc. I think the key to whether it's good or not lies in the viewer's response to a piece of design. Do they say "I've seen it before" or, "I've seen it before but not in that way."'

In other words, it is acceptable to borrow from, and be influenced by, for example, the Victorian illustrator Aubrey Beardsley, like the English psychedelic poster artists did in the late sixties, if you make something new out of it. Picasso did it with African masks – in his use of these beautiful images he performed an act of transformation that allowed us to see something new.

Allowing influences into your work is one of the ways that you expand your expressive range. Designers enrich their work – not diminish it – by looking for ways to 'incorporate' new and radical modes of expression into their work, especially from places outside contemporary design. Shutting out influences because of an obsession with 'originality' is a trap. But you have to be able to acknowledge the debt to your sources. Copyists never own up to it; the talented always do. That's the difference.

Primal Scream *XTRMNTR*
by Julian House

The brief

All design jobs start with a brief; even if it's a self-initiated project, a designer must have a brief. And the first duty of a graphic designer is to understand the brief. To do this, you must research it, question it and, if necessary, challenge it. And if, after all that, it still doesn't make sense you might need to tear it up and rewrite it. In some cases you might need to walk away from it as not all briefs are worth taking on. Learning to say no to bad briefs is a vital judgment that all designers have to learn how and when to make.

Briefs can be verbal, they can be written, and sometimes they are neither. I've had clients – usually long-standing clients – who've sent me a photograph and some text and said: 'Poster by Friday, thanks.' I suppose even that is a sort of brief: they know that I know what they want, so nothing more need be said. But this is not the usual way. It is much more common to have a written or verbal brief. Sometimes the brief is a discussion. This is okay, but it always pays to get clients to put briefs in writing: it adds clarity and it forces a thorough examination of the subject. However, some clients just don't do it. This reluctance should set off an alarm bell. It should prompt the question: is this client reliable and serious? Clients who don't brief properly are potentially dangerous. It is often their way of colonizing a job, of taking it over, of gaining the upper hand. Without a brief a designer is vulnerable, and all the power rests with the client. If a client doesn't give you a written brief, you must write one yourself and send it to back to him or her for approval. Writing your own brief from a client's instruction is a good discipline. It makes you think deeply about the project and it puts you into the mind of the client. And as we've noted in an earlier chapter, this is one of the secrets of a successful client-designer relationship.

2 It was common when
showing Intro work
at design events and art
colleges, to be asked
how we managed to get
so many 'good briefs'.
This made me splutter.
We didn't get 'good
briefs', we got the same
shoddy briefs everyone
else gets; we just made
them good by question-
ing them, challenging
them, and sometimes
disobeying them.

Most design briefs in the commercial world are shoddy, half-baked and unpromising. When these run-of-the-mill briefs come your way, you have to fight to make them into 'good briefs.' Sometimes you will fail. Sometimes you will push too hard and you will come into conflict with your client, and you will be given the boot. But on other occasions, you will succeed in turning a base-metal brief into a block of shining gold. It's all a question of attitude (allied with good communication skills and integrity). Many briefs include attempts to pre-empt the creative process. In other words, they try to do the designer's job for them. Sometimes this is an unavoidable characteristic of the job. The client knows what they want and they are saying it. But generally it is a recipe for failure. How you deal with this, and other shortcomings of the briefing process, will determine your degree of success.

The first thing you have to do is start with the premise that even a bad brief is really a good brief; assuming a sound moral and ethical base, there is no such thing as a bad brief – only a bad response. But let's assume that your client has given you a comprehensive, well-thought-out brief stating all the requirements of the job, and that you have agreed to the schedule and budget. What happens next? Well, written briefs do not preclude you from having further discussions with your client about the project. This will throw up interesting information and reveal nuances perhaps not covered in the document. It will also allow you to test your preliminary thinking on your client. Naturally, you must fully absorb the written brief; don't just concentrate on the bits you like the look of, or those bits that give you the chance to do what you do best: dig deep and look for problem areas. If you are working with a team, go through it with other members of the team, make sure you all see it in the same way (remarkably difficult to achieve, everybody gets snared and snagged on different aspects of the project). And, importantly, you must look for the 'McGuffin.'

The McGuffin was the name of a dramatic device used by Alfred Hitchcock in his movies to catch the audience's attention. The McGuffin had no real relevance to the plot: in *Psycho*, for instance, the McGuffin was Janet Leigh's theft of the money. Hitchcock used this to suck the audience into the unexpected final third of the film. I'm not suggesting you look for dramatic devices in design briefs. I'm co-opting the term (with apologies to the great Hitch) to suggest the magic component in all briefs that you have to find to explain them. In every brief there's a McGuffin that unlocks the essential nature of the task. You just have to find it.

Here's an example of what I mean. I was recently part of a team invited to pitch for the redesign of a staid real estate magazine. It was a journal for the professional sector of the UK real estate market, read by developers, investors, architects and property conglomerates. The magazine had received a full-scale graphic makeover by a leading international design company in the mid-nineties, but was now showing its age. An exhaustive and detailed brief was supplied to us. My colleagues and I sifted through the well-written document. We discussed it in detail, we analyzed it, we tried to condense it, and we looked for the McGuffin.

The brief stated that a redesign was necessary because the existing design was dated. It pointed out that various navigational improvements were required to reflect the magazine's changing editorial make-up. And it listed some requirements concerning the accommodation of new features and advertising. The brief went into copious and helpful detail about its readership and its competitors on the news stands. But we couldn't find the McGuffin.

It was only in discussion with the magazine's art director and editor that the McGuffin was identified. The property market, it was explained, had changed dramatically since the mid-nineties. It used to be a business for rich men with cigars, pinstripe suits and Rolls-Royces. Today, it has become a much less formal business; it is populated by younger people of both sexes, many of whom wear casual clothes to work, and who value design (interior design, architecture and graphic design) as an essential part of the property-development process. We'd noticed that printed literature and billboards put up by real estate companies and developers had become 'sexy'. The property world, we noticed, had woken up to good design.

Here was our McGuffin: the magic equation that gave us our winning formula. We based our response on the idea that the magazine's new design had to combine informality with high contemporary style while continuing to function as a digest of news and comment, with its attendant production and editorial demands. In our presentation, we convinced the publisher, the editor, the advertising manager and the art director that this was the right answer.

Every brief has its McGuffin; the designer's job is to find it. Sometimes it's there already, identified and isolated by the client. No need to search for it, it's staring you in the face. But more often it is absent. Experience helps you find it, but so does diligence and research and asking questions. If you don't find it, you are unlikely to produce a great piece of rounded work.

Sometimes briefs are simply wrong, and it is occasionally necessary to disobey them. 'Wrong' briefs make assumptions and outline premises that are incorrect, feeble or short-sighted. When you spot this, you have a choice. You can rewrite the brief; you can walk away from it; or you can do what is asked of you. There's yet another option, and that is to *disobey* the brief and do what you think is right. With this approach you risk everything: you risk incurring the client's displeasure, and you risk being sacked from a project or thrown off a pitch list. But if you are confident that you are right, and you can live with the consequences, it's worth following your instinct and being disobedient.

There is the most spectacular example of disobeying a 'wrong' brief, in the work of Bruno Monguzzi, the great Swiss designer. Monguzzi was called in by the Musée d'Orsay in Paris, after a design competition had failed to produce a winning poster with which to launch the newly opened museum. Monguzzi was instructed to design a poster avoiding pictorial imagery and using only two elements: the museum logo (which Monguzzi had designed) and the date. Monguzzi describes his response:

9 décembre 1986

Musée d'Orsay, Paris, opening poster by Bruno Monguzzi.
Photograph: Jacques-Henri Lartigue

'So here I was at home with a new brief and began to endlessly play around with the date and the logo, the logo and the date, getting nowhere. Nothing was happening, nothing was opening, nothing was beginning. I walked over to my books, picked up a [Henri] Lartigue album, and slowly began to go through the pages. When I came to the image of his brother taking off with a glider that their uncle had constructed at chateau Rouzat, I knew I had the answer. The fly had broken the web.

'And here I was, back in Paris again, with Jean Jenger [the director] and Leone Nora [public relations], knowing I had disobeyed. I was using a photograph, and no image was to be used. Jenger got very upset. He said that we had all agreed that no work of art should appear on the poster. And that anyway it was not *le musée de l'aviation.*"

'I said that it was a metaphor and that the people that knew the logo knew what the museum was all about. I nevertheless added that the poster had to be their poster. That it should belong to them. But Jenger had stopped listening and began to talk to himself pacing nervously up and down the room. I tried to interrupt him, asserting that he did not have to convince me. He said he was thinking. My eyes met the eyes of Madame Nora, which were a bit perplexed, but very beautiful, and we sat down.

'Jenger would sometimes stop, look at the poster, and then start his gymnastics all over again. I think he was trying to imagine the possible reactions of all the people he really or virtually knew. A kind of French human comedy with an unexpected end. "Monguzzi," he said, "I am so convinced that the poster is right, that I will bring it myself to Rigaud" [the president of the museum]. The following day a worried Madame Nora was on the phone. The Lartigue Foundation does not allow the cropping of Lartigue's photographs. Not knowing which way to turn I asked her to try showing the project to the Foundation anyway. Not only were we allowed to use the photograph as planned, but a vintage print of that shot was given to the museum. It was the fourth Lartigue to enter the collection.'[3]

3   Taken from Bruno Monguzzi, *A Designer's Perspective*, Baltimore: The Fine Arts Gallery. 1998.

There are three important lessons to be gleaned from this extract. The first is that it is sometimes necessary to disobey a brief when you know it to be wrong. It was clear that the museum director was wrong – or at best short-sighted – to prohibit the use of pictorial imagery and impose restrictions on the designer. (It almost certainly explains why the competition entries were all regarded as worthless – they'd followed the brief and were consequently bloodless and ineffectual.) But by disregarding the brief, Monguzzi produced an enduring piece of work that would have had much less impact if he'd followed his client's instructions which effectively neutered him.

The second lesson is less obvious. In this account of his experience of designing a poster, Monguzzi illustrates the need to give new work time to become assimilated by the client. As I pointed out in the chapter devoted to clients, designers often expect instant responses to their work. We are impatient and demand immediate approval, when what clients need is time to absorb and reflect. The client brings his or her own expectations to any work they are seeing for the first time. These expectations have to be sifted through before an objective and considered response can be formulated. The museum director went from disapproval to enthusiastic acceptance, but he didn't do it instantly. And Monguzzi knew to give him time.

The final lesson is less quantifiable than the previous two. Monguzzi's story goes some way towards proving a rather misty-eyed theory of mine, which is that when a work of design is right, no matter how challenging and off-brief it may appear, it will win acceptance. I admit to a bit of designer utopianism here, and we could have an interesting debate about what 'right' means in this context. And yes, I know designers will point to cabinets full of rejected work and say 'I did this brilliant design and look, it got rejected.' But, I still believe that when we get it right, when we create something that is in every way correct, it is recognized even by the most dim-witted clients. Monguzzi's story comes close to proving my rickety theory.

Self-initiated briefs

The notion of self-initiated briefs – graphic authorship, as it is often called – currently occupies a prominent position in design discourse. In my view, self-initiated projects and the notion of 'pure' graphic authorship are well intentioned but flawed as concepts. Graphic designers need briefs. A graphic designer who doesn't need a brief isn't a graphic designer: he or she might be an artist or a metaphysical poet, but they're not graphic designers. The need for a brief is hard-wired into the designer's psyche. In fact, although designers constantly demand freedom, they really crave constraint. It's a little recognized fact, but designers are only happy when they are battling with restraints. Of course, many designers like to erect their own barriers and live by their own rules, and a natural offshoot of this is the desire for self-authored briefs. But this shouldn't be confused with pure authorship: all it means is that designers are combining the role of client and designer. I'm not decrying the notion of self-initiated projects. I am saying, however, that the graphic designer's mentality is suited, thanks to education, temperament and tradition, to responding to a brief. Perhaps there will emerge a new superstrain of mutant designers who have evolved beyond the point of needing a brief; but I doubt it.

The commonly held view is that designers need briefs because designers are problem solvers. I don't like the term 'problem solvers'; it seems to play into the hands of those who see design as a purely mechanistic process – although it must be said that many of the best designers consider themselves to be 'problem solvers', and produce resonant and lasting work accordingly. But my feeling is that the term 'problem solver' only defines one part of what designers do, and often denies the aesthetic nature of design (it doesn't matter what it looks like as long as it 'solves the problem'). [4] Designers need briefs like cars need fuel: they don't work otherwise. Designers who work from briefs are still authors, but it's authorship in the sense that they have created something in response to a set of defined requirements and taken into account a number of relevant conditions (purpose, commercial considerations, budget, time, media channels, etc.).

4   You see this most clearly in advertising. Graphic design in advertising is secondary to 'the idea.' I was once shown a range of famous advertising posters by an advertising man: he showed them to make the point that in all cases, the idea (the message) was instantly graspable. I pointed out to him that not one of these posters could be said to be well designed. He agreed, but he didn't care.

Research

Before starting a new project, designers frequently go off into a corner with a favorite pile of books (usually the same ones as last time) and skim through them looking for ideas. Nothing wrong with this. We all do it. We're not necessarily setting out to copy ideas; we're looking for triggers to set off a chain reaction of inspiration. But it is a good idea to try and find different sources for inspiration; it is a good idea to look for triggers in unlikely places.

Research is easier now than it once was. The Internet puts a Niagara Falls of data at our fingertips. It's easy to find information on any subject. Knowledge is power: the more we know, the better we function, and that's true whether you are a street cleaner or a designer. However, looking for – and finding – inspiration is not the same as doing research. I mentioned at the beginning of this book that cultural awareness was one of the prime attributes of the modern designer. Cultural awareness, when it's backed up with specifically targeted research, is the high-octane fuel that drives great ideas. Careful research can open up creative possibilities that would otherwise remain locked to us. It is also vital that designers do research if only to provide rationales for their work. As I've already noted, it's not good enough to say: 'I've done it this way because I like it.' You have to have a reason, and that reason has to be objective.

Clients often urge designers to 'study the competition.' If a company asks you to design their website, they will probably suggest that you look at the websites of their competitors. Nothing wrong with this, designers should certainly study the activities of their client's competitors. But it's worth remembering that your client is probably encouraging you to look at the competition so that you will create something that 'looks like' the competition. For some designers, this is acceptable: they regard themselves as professional servants and are happy to oblige. For the independent-minded graphic designer, however, this is anathema. Yet, it is only by studying the sites of your client's competitors that you will have the ammunition to argue your case for making a strong and original execution. Clients have a herd instinct (many designers have too) and if you want to do original and distinctive work, you will need to break this down, and you can only do this with high-end creativity backed up by well-researched argument.

One piece of research that designers often omit – with disastrous consequences – is that they don't bother to read the text they are asked to design. Now, designers are often supplied with feeble texts in the first place, nevertheless, you are not going to create anything with any lasting merit unless you read it, and respond by coaxing out its true meaning with sympathetic typography and layout. This is a tough lesson and I only learned it when I started to write about design myself. I saw the way that some publications took great care over the way my texts were presented, while others simply flowed it in giving no thought to line breaks, hyphenation, leading and all the other subtleties that make up meaningful design. Do you want to know how to be a great typographer? Learn to handle text by writing text yourself and then laying it out. Nothing sharpens up the typographer's eye more than sweating over the composition of a 2,000-word essay and then rendering it typographically; just as few things sting as cruelly as writing 2,000 words and then seeing your efforts destroyed by crass, unsympathetic typography. This simple experiment – write your own text and then lay it out – will transform your perspective on typography and layout instantly.

Process

Graphic design is now almost entirely a digital activity. Indeed, if you want it to be, design can be 100 per cent digital: as a designer you need never again hold a pencil or develop a photographic print from a negative, or create a font by hand. It can all be done with a computer. The computer has revolutionized the design process. It has made the act of designing *easier*, and in many ways it has improved the way we design things. Yet in other respects it has made design more formulaic, and it has standardized the act of designing. Before computers, designers worked in ways that suited them temperamentally. Some operated surrounded by piles of paper, books, type-specimen sheets and drafting equipment, using pencils and markers to map out fluid design concepts. Others worked within strictly controlled parameters using methodical precision to create structured and rational work. Some stood at drawing boards, while others sat crouched over their work like Victorian ledger clerks. Today, thanks to speed-of-light microprocessors and do-everything software, we all design in the same way: we sit lifelessly, only our wrists moving, as we stare at a screen. Our focus has narrowed. We rarely look at our work from a distance. We rarely look at it from different angles. We often work in miniature. We avoid anything that can't be done 'on' the computer. The screen dictates our relationship to our work – it dictates how our work looks.

I'm not anti-computer. Far from it. The computer enables us to do *more* work, and it enables us to operate with greater technical proficiency. It can't do everything, but it has freed the designer from drudgery, and it has brought within the grasp of any designer who can afford a computer modes of graphic expression that were once nearly impossible to achieve, because of cost or technical complexity. The computer is a good thing. No question about it. But with the computer has come a set of problems that, virus-like, infect the actual process of design. What used to be slow and methodical is now fast and often slipshod: ask a designer to produce some logo ideas and you'll get dozens of versions in roughly the time it takes to think them into existence.

The computer allows the designer to explore countless options. Before computers, you had to trace off letterforms, or hand-render text, or represent pictures with magic-marker sketches; it might take an entire morning to render a headline, or days to prepare a mock-up of a typographic layout, or months to create a typeface. Neville Brody tells the story of the epiphany-like moment when he saw, for the first time, Fontographer being used to create a font. Up until this point, Brody had been laboriously drawing alphabets by hand (as had been the case for centuries), but now here was a way that meant it could be done in a fraction of the time. Brody became a digital convert. He was among the first high-profile converts to the computer in design.

But with speed of execution comes another prob-
lem – a very digital problem. With the ability to produce so much
work, it's harder to know whether what you are doing is any
good. Ian Anderson, the self-taught graphic designer and
founder of The Designers Republic, was asked if he ever had
designers block. Anderson replied: 'My problem in that area,
and it sounds an arrogant thing to say, is there are too many
ideas, and information overload. Then it's how do I get everything I want to say into this thing. I can't remember a time when
I didn't know what to do or didn't know how to do it. It's much
more about which route to take. If you have a block you should
just walk around it or start your own journey from a different
place. Looking at something in a different way requires the discipline of giving up what you already have. Sometimes the only
way to move forward is to dump everything and start again.
Then you will find the work you have already completed helps
inform your new direction.' 5

S Book 2, edited by
Nick Long,
Art Books International,
5   2004.

Anderson has touched on a uniquely digital problem facing the contemporary
designer. He is talking about the importance of the designer's role as 'editor'. Editing is the
great skill of the digital era. Now that we can produce a surfeit of everything, the ability to
know what to 'retain' and what to 'discard' is essential. In the digital domain you can have
everything you want (as Anderson says: 'too many ideas' or 'information overload'). With
digital cameras we can incorporate images within seconds; we can scan anything that can
be fitted onto a scanner; we can have any typeface, any effect, and we can have it now. So
when Anderson talks about taking alternative 'routes'; starting journeys from a 'different
place'; dumping everything and starting again, he is really talking about editing.

How do you edit? You have to ask yourself a few questions. Is the work true to
your philosophy of what constitutes good design? In other words, does the work have
integrity? To be a good editor, you also need time and distance. By all means create thirty
logos before lunch time, but don't send them until the following day. Print them out, pin them
on the wall, and go home. Come back the next day, and you will see things that you didn't
see yesterday. Ask friends and other designers what they think.

This is editing: filtering your work to eliminate the feeble and promote the remarkable. Never show thirty logos to a client; of those thirty you designed, show only three, or at
most four versions. Showing more shows you to be indecisive (no editing skills) and creates
a picture of graphic design as a shotgun process. If you are really brave and confident show
only the one you think is best (remember not to say you've done it because you like it); but
it's usually better to show three versions covering three different angles of approach.

Ian Anderson also alludes to another process that is a direct by-product of the digital way of working: iteration. Digital tools allow the designer to 'iterate' on a grand scale.
'Thirty logos by end of the day? No problem. Color and mono versions in varying sizes? No
problem. They'll be loaded onto an FTP site by 5 pm. Call me when you've seen them.' This is
business in real time. It's what the modern world is about. If you can't do thirty logos by 5 pm
for your client in Singapore (you're in Seattle) someone else will. But hang on, what about
quality? The iterative process means that you can work your way through countless options,
but unless you are applying careful editing powers as you go, you will end up with a soup of
indifferent ideas, remarkable only for their plentifulness. Modern designers must use the gift

of iteration to work towards a conclusion rather than as an opportunity to explore every known avenue. In the pre-digital era, the designer had to think harder about the final destination, because iteration wasn't possible on any scale. Few of us would go back to that way of working, but we nevertheless must learn to structure our work so that we progress in a straight line rather than a serpentine loop that never arrives anywhere.

Nor must we be frightened of failure. All great endeavours flirt with failure at some point in their existence. Only the irredeemably bland avoids looking into the abyss. The great writer and semiotician Umberto Eco, writing about contemporary processes of scientific discovery said: 'Modern science does not hold that what is new is always right. On the contrary, it is based on the principle of "fallibilism" … according to which science progresses by continually correcting itself, falsifying its hypotheses by trial and error, admitting its own mistakes – and by considering that an experiment that doesn't work out is not a failure but is worth as much as a successful one because it proves that a certain line of research was mistaken and it is necessary either to change direction or even to start over from scratch.'

'Fallibilism' should be the guiding principle for all graphic designers. When the designer falls back on existing templates of thinking, and habitual visual reflexes and patterns, sterility is the result. It is only by daring to experiment, and by taking risks, that rich and meaningful design is created. This is especially so in the digital domain, where fallibilism becomes doubly relevant. The computer, with its speed-of-thought processing power, enables the designer to explore and execute ideas with a twist of the wrist. But there is no advantage in this ability to experiment if we don't use it as an opportunity to leap into the void.

Criteria for good work

What constitutes good work? For one designer, a hand-painted sign on the side of a fruit stall in Mumbai is the pinnacle of graphic excellence. For another, it is the modular typography of Wim Crouwel. For yet another, it's the street-swagger of well-executed graffiti. These are aesthetic questions, and as such are personal to the individual designer – and, of necessity, to the designer's client and audience. The answer will always be subjective. I'm not going to tell you which of these I think is best, but I can give you some practical criteria for evaluating your own work. There are three questions to ask yourself at the end of every job. Is the client happy? Is the job profitable? Is the project newsworthy?

I'm afraid these seem depressingly prosaic when spelled out baldly like this. Has all your hard work, your idealism, your love of design, come down to this? Well, I'm afraid to say the answer is at least partly, yes. But, let's look at these three conditions, they may be blunt and mundane, but they are stepping stones on the way to enlightenment.

1   Is the client happy? Pretty crucial when you think about it. If the client isn't happy you've got problems. You may have executed a great piece of work, it might even occupy the prime spot in your portfolio, but if your client isn't happy with it you might be in trouble. At worst, it might mean that you don't get paid: if it's a big job, with a large fee involved, perhaps substantial outside costs, this can be catastrophic. It might also mean that you don't get any more work from that client. It will almost certainly mean that you won't get any recommendations or referrals from that client. And perhaps most painful of all, you will know that you have failed as a graphic designer. By the nature of design we are obliged to make our clients happy. To fail to do this is to fail as a graphic designer.

2   Is the job profitable? By profitable, I mean both in the financial sense and in the non-monetary sense. In other words, you might do a job for a charity or for a not-for-profit organization, or you might do it because it is a job that will 'profit' you in terms of exposure and recognition. The profit in all these cases is not financial. Rather it is to do with an intellectual or an intangible profit, such as the satisfaction that comes from helping others. But, in the term's strictly financial sense, it means not losing money on a job and showing a cash profit. If you want to survive in the design business and be able to pay your taxes, your staff and yourself, you are going to have to show a profit on most of your jobs, not necessarily on every job, but you are going to have to make more money than you spend. Capitalism may not be perfect, but it has a blunt simplicity that, at least, is easily grasped by the financially unsophisticated.

3   Is the project newsworthy? What I'm talking about here is your work's ability to attract attention, and, as a consequence of that attention, attract other work. In the current design scene nothing succeeds like success. It gets people talking (word of mouth), it excites journalists and commentators (exposure) and it wins awards and gets published in books and exhibitions (recognition). Of course, to succeed as a designer, you need to be efficient, pleasant to work with and utterly professional. But this alone will only get you so far. What really lights the fuse is great work.

Many designers would add a fourth category to this list. What about 'suitability for the intended audience,' they might ask. And rightly so, after all, we design not for ourselves or our clients, but for our audience. But the problem about having this as an evaluation criterion is that designers rarely get to see or meet their audiences. We don't often get to meet the people who are the recipients of our work, other than by accident. We have few ways, beyond intuition and common sense, of evaluating the success of our work with its intended audience. We can have anecdotal evidence, and we catch glimpses of its effects from time to time, and we get feedback (especially in the interactive domain, where users can post their responses), but all this is haphazard and unscientific. Audience acceptance is usually covered in the reaction of our clients. If we produce design that flops our client will let us know, and we certainly won't be able to tick box number one as a result.

The three criteria I've listed above *can* be personally evaluated. We can get answers to the questions they pose. And if we want to evaluate our work, and test its worth, we need to ask those three questions every time we complete a project. If you can tick any one of the three boxes you are doing well. If you can tick any two you are doing better. If you can tick all three boxes, you've won first prize in graphic design's metaphorical lottery. Of course, there are jobs where you can't tick any of the boxes. We all get those jobs, real stinkers where you end up with nothing but the lingering stench of failure. But you must learn from these jobs when they happen, because even among all the debris there will be valuable lessons to be learned: you may have improved some aspect of your functionality as a designer or as a studio; you might have acquired a new skill in order to undertake this job; you might have 'broken in' a new designer (or client) who will do better next time. But what I've described above are the three main considerations – by no means the only ones – for evaluating a completed project.

How to be a graphic designer

After reading this book you will perhaps become a design superhero – although it must be said that turning designers into superheroes was not one of my intentions when I sat down to write this book. In fact, the notion of design superheroes is mildly repellent, and not in any way related to the spirit that drove me to write this book. My intentions were much more modest.

My only hope is that you are now better equipped to deal with life as a graphic designer. The subject is vast, and I can only aspire to dealing with one tiny sliver of the cake. I haven't talked about design theory or the minutiae of practice life (job numbers, project management or tax planning). There are better people to tell you about these subjects, and I've provided a bibliography with recommendations for further reading. But just as research and inquisitiveness should be a big part of your life as a designer, so should a willingness to learn. When I started life as a designer it seemed to me to be the most exciting job in the world. I still feel that. There's something uniquely privileged and stimulating about having a job where you know you will have an effect (however slight) on the lives of others; there's something magical about doing something that might be seen by millions; and there's something exhilarating about having a job where you get to make a mark.

The biggest problem designers face is fear: fear of clients, fear of failure, fear of ideas. Our ability to overcome fear is perhaps the greatest skill we can acquire. Most bad design, most mediocre design, is a consequence of fear. Clients are frightened; designers are frightened; audiences are frightened. The modern world of commerce runs on fear: a marketplace terror that makes us timid and risk-averse. Most of us deal with fear by falling back on the familiar and the safe. But if we do this, we are not allowed to turn round and say our lives are dull. If we are going to avoid losing our souls, we have to overcome the fear.

John Biggs,
Basic Typography
London:
Faber and Faber, 1968.

Michael Bierut, William Drenttel,
Steven Heller, eds.,
Looking Closer 2:
Critical Writings on Graphic Design
New York:
Allworth Press, 1997.

Michael Bierut, Jessica Helfand,
Steven Heller, Rick Poynor, eds.,
Looking Closer 3:
Critical Writings on Graphic Design
New York:
Allworth Press, 1999.

Lewis Blackwell, Neville Brody,
G1:
New Dimensions in Graphic Design
London:
Laurence King Publishing, 1996.

Lewis Blackwell,
Twentieth-Century Type
London:
Laurence King Publishing, 2004.

Robert Bringhurst,
The Elements of Typographic Style
Vancouver:
Hartney And Marks Publishers, 1992.

David Crow,
Visible Signs
Switzerland:
AVA Publishing SA, 2003.

Dave Eggers,
A Heartbreaking
Work of Staggering Genius
New York:
Simon and Schuster, 2000.

Cameron Foote,
The Creative Business Guide to
Running A Graphic Design Business
New York:
WW Norton, 2004.

Roz Goldfarb,
Careers By Design, A Business
Guide for Graphic Designers
New York,
Watson Guptill, 2002.

Dorothy Goslett,
The Professional Practice of Design
London:
Batsford, 1971.

Peter Hall,
Sagmeister
London:
Booth-Clibborn Editions, 2001.

Steven Heller,
Design Literacy (Continued),
Understanding Graphic Design
New York:
Allworth Press, 1999.

Steven Heller,
The Graphic Design Reader
New York:
Allworth Press, 2002.

Steven Heller, ed.,
The Education of a Typographer
New York:
Allworth Press, 2004.

Steven Heller and Elinor Pettit, (eds).,
Design Dialogues
New York:
Allworth Press, 1998.

Steven Heller and
Philip B Meggs (eds).,
Texts on Type:
Critical Writings on Typography
New York:
Allworth Press, 2001.

Steven Heller and
Veronique Vienne (eds).,
Citizen Designer
New York:
Allworth Press, 2003.

Richard Hollis,
Graphic Design: A Concise History
London:
Thames and Hudson, 1997.

Intro,
Sampler:
Contemporary Music Graphics
London:
Laurence King Publishing, 1999.

Intro,
Sampler 2:
Art, Pop and Contemporary
Music Graphics
London:
Laurence King Publishing, 2000.

Intro,
Sampler 3:
Radical Album Cover Art
London:
Laurence King Publishing, 2003.

Emily King, ed.,
Designed by Peter Saville
New York:
Princeton Architectural Press, 2003.

Andy Law,
Experiment at Work
London:
Profile Books, 2003.

Ellen Lupton,
Thinking with Type:
A Critical Guide for Designers,
Writers, Editors, Students
New York:
Princeton Architectural Press, 2004.

Robyn Marsack,
Essays On Design 1:
AGI's Designers of Influence
London:
Booth-Clibborn Editions, 1997.

Bruno Monguzzi,
A Designer's Perspective
Baltimore:
The Fine Arts Gallery, 1998.

Quentin Newark,
What is Graphic Design?
Brighton:
Rotovision, 2002.

Peter Noever, ed.,
Stefan Sagmeister Handarbeit
Vienna:
MAK, 2002.

Donald Norman,
The Design of Everyday Things
Cambridge, MA:
MIT Press, 1998.

Peter Phillips,
Creating The Perfect Design Brief:
How To Manage Design For Strategic
Advantage
New York:
Allworth Press, 2004.

Sergio Polano, Pierpaolo Vetta,
ABC of 20th Century Graphics
Milan:
Electa Architecture, 2003.

Virginia Postrel,
The Substance of Style
New York:
HarperCollins, 2003.

Norman Potter,
What Is A Designer
London:
Hyphen Press, 2002.

Christine Poulson, ed.,
*William Morris
on Art and Design*
Sheffield:
Sheffield Academic Press, 1996.

Rick Poynor,
*Design Without Boundaries:
Visual Communication in Transition*
London:
Booth-Clibborn Editions, 1998.

Rick Poynor,
*Obey the Giant:
Life in the Image World*
London:
August Media, 2001.

Rick Poynor,
*No More Rules:
Graphic Design and Post-Modernism*
London:
Laurence King Publishing, 2003.

Rick Poynor, ed.,
*Communicate: Independent
Graphic Design Since the Sixties*
London:
Laurence King Publishing, 2004.

Jonas Ridderstrale, Kjelle Nordstrom,
Funky Business
Harlow:
Pearson Education, 2002.

Ricardo Semler,
Maverick!
London:
Random House Business Books,
1999.

Herbert Spencer,
Pioneers of Modern Typography
Hampshire:
Lund Humphries, 2004.

A Tomato Project,
Process
London:
Thames and Hudson, 1996.

A Tomato Project,
Bareback
London:
Laurence King Publishing, 1999.

Rudy VanderLans, ed.,
Emigre: Nudging Graphic Design
New York:
Princeton Architectural Press,
2003.

Rudy VanderLans, ed.,
*Emigre: If We're Standing On
The Shoulders of Giants,
What Are We Reaching for?*
New York:
Princeton Architectural Press, 2004.

Gerald Woods, Philip Thompson,
John Williams, eds.,
Art Without Boundaries
New York:
Praeger, 1972.

Organizations

Adg-fad www.adg-fad.org
Spanish Graphic Design Association

American Institute of Graphic Arts
www.aiga.org
The oldest and largest national
professional graphic design organization,
committed to promotion of excellence
in graphic design.

The Art Directors Club
www.adcglobal.org/main.html
International non-profit organization
of leading creatives across all design
disciplines.

ATypI www.atypi.org/
Association Typographique
Internationale, founded in 1975. The
premier international body
dedicated to type and typography.

Australian Graphic Design Association
www.agda.asn.au/
Non-profit organization founded to
facilitate the advancement of graphic
design as a profession in Australia.

British Design Initiative
www.britishdesign.co.uk
Agency that owns an accurate database
of UK design agencies, design
awards and professional design bodies
internationally.

Creative Latitude
www.creativelatitude.com/
Educates designers about the design
business, and helps independent
designers market themselves. Website
provides resources and business-
related Q&As.

Creative Ireland
www.creativeireland.com
Online home of the Irish design
community.

D&AD www.dandad.org
Sets creative standards, inspires
and promotes good design and
advertising in the UK.

Design Council
www.designcouncil.org.uk
Helps people and organizations in
business, education, public services and
government understand design and
use it effectively as part of their strategy.

Design Institute
design.umn.edu/go/to/root
Based at the University of Minnesota,
the Design Institute commissions,
publishes and implements innovative
design ideas for the public realm and
hosts a variety of public programming.

Graphic Artist's Guild
www.gag.org/
National union of illustrators, designers
and other creative disciplines.
Publishes a handbook guide to pricing
and ethical guidelines.

Icograda www.icograda.org
International Council of Graphic Design
Associations is the professional
world body for graphic design and visual
communication. A voluntary coming
together of associations concerned with
graphic design, design management,
design promotion and design education.

Letter Exchange

www.letterexchange.org/index.html
Society for professionals involved in the
lettering arts and crafts, from calligraphy
and letter-cutting, through design
for print, publishing and typography, to
signage and architectural lettering.

MIT Media Lab

www.media.mit.edu/
Focuses on how electronic information
overlaps with the everyday physical
world. This research body explores the
study, invention and creative use of
digital technologies to enhance the ways
that people think, express and
communicate ideas, and explore new
scientific frontiers.

Premsela: Dutch Design Foundation

www.premselastichting.org/home/-/en
An organization concentrating on the
cultural significance of Dutch
design nationally and internationally.

Society of Graphic Designers of Canada

www.gdc.net/
Member-based organization of design
professionals, educators, administrators,
students, and associates in
communications, marketing, media and
design-related fields.

Society of Illustrators

www.societyillustrators.org/
National organization comprised
of professional artists in the fields of
illustration, cartooning, animation,
graphic design and allied fields.

Society of Publication Designers

www.spd.org/
A driving force for quality and innovation
in publication design; they specifically
address the concerns of trade, corporate,
institutional, newspaper and consumer
editorial art directors.

Tokyo Type Directors Club

www.tdctokyo.org/
Primary activities include an annual
international design competition, the
publication of a yearbook
and production of exhibitions.

Ecological Design Association

www.edaweb.org
Non-profit-making registered charity
launched by David Pearson,
architect and author of *The Natural
House Book*, and others.

ISTD www.istd.org.uk
International Society of Typographic
Designers establishes and maintains
typographic standards within the design
and education communities, through
the forum of debate and design, and by
publishing and promoting the
highest quality contemporary practice
among its international membership.

The Organisation of Black Designers

www.core77.com/obd/
Non-profit professional association
dedicated to promoting the visibility,
education, empowerment and
interaction of its membership, and the
understanding and value that diverse
design perspectives contribute to world
culture and commerce.

SOTA www.typesociety.org/
The Society of Typographic Aficionados
is a non-profit organization devoted
to type, typography and the related arts.

Business matters

Business Link
www.businesslink.gov.uk
Clearly explained government-run
guide to new and existing businesses
in the UK.

Enterprise
forum.europa.eu.int/irc/sme/euroinforma
tion/info/data/sme/en/sis/gsi.html
General start-up information for
businesses within the European Union.

Inc.com
www.inc.com/guides/start_biz/
Abundance of practical advice for new
businesses with extensive How to Start a
Business section.

Internet Business Planner
www.cbsc.org/ibp/home_en.cfm
Free business planning software
designed to operate on the World Wide
Web. The IBP uses the capabilities
of the internet to assist in preparing
three-year business plan for their new or
existing business.

Strategis
www.
strategis.ic.gc/engdoc/mainb.html
Site giving information on starting a
business in Canada.

United States Small Business
Administration
www.sba.gov/startingbusiness/
planning/basic.html
Helpful and informative guide to
start-up basics, including advice on
business planning, financing,
marketing. employees, taxes, etc.

Conferences

AIGA
www.aiga.org/content.cfm/
conferences
The American Institute of Graphic Arts
sponsors a number of different
conferences on design education,
design and business and current issues
in design.

Grafic Europe
www.graficeurope.com
Comprehensive annual conference
for the pan-European graphic design
community.

How Conference
www.howconference.com/
How magazine's annual creativity,
business and technology conference
for graphic designers.

International Design Conference Aspen
www.idca.org/
Begun in 1951, the IDCA examines the
designed environment in the context
of the arts, sciences and the humanities.

Profile Intermedia
www.magni7icent.net/
Europe's most unconventional,
diverse, unique and inspirational design
and media festival.

Internet resources

Adbusters
www.adbusters.org/
Global network of artists, activists,
writers, pranksters, students, educators
and entrepreneurs who want to
advance the new social activist
movement of the information age.

Back Space   www.backspace.com
Notes on the built environment, graphic
design, product design, architecture,
the decisions we make, and the impact
they have.

Boxes and Arrows
www.boxesandarrows.com/
Definitive source for the task of bringing
architecture and design to the digital
landscape.

Computer Love
www.computerlove.net/
Hyperactive site for the digitally inclined.

The Department of Typography
& Graphic Communication
www.rdg.ac.uk/Typography/home.html?
staff/academic/erick.html
For more than thirty years, the
Department of Typography & Graphic
Communication at Reading
University has been the only one of its
kind in a British university.

Design is Kinky
www.designiskinky.net/
Global meeting place and notice board
for design activities of all kinds.

Design Observer
www.designobserver.com/
Online blog with design's intellectual
pacesetters leading from the front:
Michael Bierut, William Drenttel, Jessica
Helfand and Rick Poynor.

Dictionary.com
dictionary.reference.com/
Invaluable online dictionary for the
working designer.

Dot Dot Dot   www.dot-dot-dot.nl
Magazine which describes itself as 'a
jocuserious fanzine-journal-orphanage …'

Eye   www.eyemagazine.com
The doyenne of design mags.

Kaliber10000   www.k10k.net/
An independent, non-commercial web zine.

The Knowledge Circuit
design.umn.edu/go/to/kc
A site that scans design and new media
conferences around the world,
tracking emerging ideas and
practitioners in all design disciplines.

kottke.org   www.kottke.org/
Jason Kottke has maintained this popular
and influential weblog since March 1998,
writing about web technology,
photography, media, network science,
design, the writable web, and rip/mix/
burn culture.

Lars Müller Publishers
www.lars-muller-publishers.com
Swiss publisher and designer Lars Müller
produces carefully edited and designed
publications on architecture, design and
contemporary photography.

Mark Holt Design   www.markholtdesign.com
Founding partner, 8vo, now running site
selling rare design books and posters.

Onedotzero   www.onedotzero.com/
Inspirational international festival of moving
image. Home to leading experimental
digital film-makers.

Our Type   www.ourtype.com/
European typography site, run by Dutch
type designer Fred Smeijers.

The Sorrell Foundation
www.thesorrellfoundation.com/
home.html
Aims to inspire creativity in young people and
to improve quality of life through good design.

Speak up

www.underconsideration.
com/speakup/
Noisy, vigorous blog, run by the
tireless Armin Vit. Less patrician than
Design Observer.

St Bride Printing Library

www.stbride.org/
Foremost printing and graphic arts
library, a role it combines with
that of a technical library serving the
UK's sixth-largest industry.

Thinking with Type

www. thinkingwithtype.com/
Witty and informative companion to the
book *Thinking with Type: A Critical
Guide for Designers, Writers, Editors,
& Students*, by Ellen Lupton.

Typotheque

www.typotheque.com/index.php
Type foundry upholding the traditions of
independent type foundries in the online
domain.

Wikipedia en.wikipedia.org/
The free encyclopedia.

YCN (Young Creatives Network)

www.ycnonline.com/
Member-based organization aiming to
inspire and showcase emerging design
and communication excellence and to
connect it with the creative industries.

YouWorkForThem

youworkforthem.com/
Sells books, magazines, videos,
CD-ROMs, T-shirts and the
best in contemporary design from
around the world.

Designers

April Greiman aprilgreiman.com/
Leading US designer and digital pioneer.

Barnbrook Design

www.barnbrook.net
Online home of UK designer Jonathan
Barnbrook's studio.

Bruce Mau

www.brucemaudesign.com
Leading Toronto-based designer.

Cyan www.cyan.de
Inspirational Berlin studio famous
for its print and moving-image work in the
cultural sector.

The Designers Republic

www.thedesignersrepublic.com/
Famous Sheffield-based iconoclasts.

Fons M Hickmann

www.kairos.to/html/fons/door.html
German typographer.

Graphic Thought Facility

www.graphicthoughtfacility.com/
British graphic design of the
highest order.

Hi-Res! www.hi-res.net/
One of the leading international
web-design companies.

John Maeda

www.maedastudio.com/
Paradigm shifting force in digital design.

Karlssonwilker Inc

www.karlssonwilker.com/
Iconoclastic design from New
York-based German and Icelandic
designers.

m/m paris www.mmparis.com/
Mould-breaking French designers.

Nakajima Design www.nkjm-d.com/
Wonderful Japanese graphic designer
and art director, Hideki Nakajima.

Non Format www.non-format.com/
London-based Innovative duo,
designers of *The Wire* magazine, among
other things.

Pentagram www.pentagram.com/
The last of the independents.
Established in the 1960s and still
producing unrivaled work.

Pleix www.pleix.net/
Virtual community of digital artists based
in Paris. View their films online.

Practise www.practise.co.uk/
The site of English designer
James Goggin.

Tandoori Yokoo www.tadanoriyokoo.com/
One of the world's great poster artists.

Vier5 www.vier5.de/
Visionary French typographers.

Cultural awareness

Arts & Letters Daily www.aldaily.com/
Encyclopedic compendium of cultural
and arts news from around the world.

Chicks on Speed
www.chicksonspeed.com/tv
Visual indigestion on this high
octane site.

Militant Aesthetics
www.militantesthetix.co.uk/

Critical Art Ensemble www.critical-art.net/
Artist collective exploring intersections
between art, technology, radical politics
and critical theory.

Guardian Unlimited
www.guardian.co.uk/
Best daily newspaper on the web.
Original site design by Neville Brody.

Internet Archive www.archive.org/
A digital library of internet sites and other
cultural artefacts in digital form.

New York Review of Books
www.nybooks.com/index
Online version of 'the premier literary-
intellectual magazine in the English
language'.

The Onion www.theonion.com/.html
Calls itself 'America's finest news source'
– which of course it is.

Resonance FM www.resonancefm.com/
London's first radio art station.

This is a magazine
www.thisisamagazine.com/
Charming and innovative online/
offline zine.

Turux www.turux.org/
Marvel of visionary web design.

WPS1 www.wps1.org/
Daily, twenty-four-hour stream of music,
talk and historic spoken-word programs
focusing on contemporary art, music and
literature from around the world.

The Wire www.thewire.co.uk/
Adventures in modern music.

Dedicated to Lynda S

Thanks to Intro friends, without whom this book would be only three pages long:
Katy Richardson, Julian Gibbs, Kate Dawkins, Mat Cook, Julian House, Adrian Talbot, Jo Marsh,
Nikki Hildesley, Melissa Robertson, Steff Holingshead and everyone else who I shared fifteen
astonishing years with.

Thanks to This is Real Art for allowing me to be semi-detached during the writing of
this book: Georgina Lee, Kate Nielsen, Sam Renwick, Sarah Withers and all the TiRA artists
and designers.

Thanks to my interviewees who pretended not to mind my nagging and cajoling: Neville Brody,
Natalie Hunter, John Warwicker, Kim Hiorthøy, Corey Holms, Rudy VanderLans, Andy Cruz,
Angela Lorenz, Peter Stemmler and Alexander Gelman.

Thanks to the people who donated images, quotes and advice: Michael C Place,
Chris Ashworth, Jonathan Ellery, Malcolm Garrett, Bruno Monguzzi, Michele Jannuzzi and
everyone else.

Thanks to all the editors and commissioners who encouraged me in my desire to write
about design: Patrick Burgoyne, Lynda Relph-Knight, Caroline Roberts, Marc Valli, John L
Walters, Richard Clayton, Steven Heller, David Womack and special tip of the hat to Rick
Poynor for bravely commissioning my first article.

Thanks to Laurence King, Jo Lightfoot, Felicity Awdry and Laura Willis.

Thanks to my editor Eugenia Bell for editorial intensive care above and beyond the call of duty.

Thanks to Jonathon Jeffrey, Mason Wells and Tim Beard at Bibliothèque for the ravishing
layout, and Mason's frequent lectures on the principles of good design.

Special thanks to Stefan Sagmeister, the patron saint of this book.

Love to Ed, Alice and Moll.